SUSHI AT HOME

Yuki Gomi is a Japanese chef who has taught thousands of people Japanese cooking and how to make their own sushi. After studying cordon bleu cookery in Chicago, she trained under Japanese master chefs, before moving to London and beginning to teach Japanese cooking classes. *Sushi at Home* is her first book.

www.yukiskitchen.com

Yuki Gomi

SUSHI AT HOME

The Beginner's Guide to Perfect,
Simple Sushi

Photography by Keiko Oikawa

PENGUIN
FIG TREE

FIG TREE

Published by the Penguin Group
Penguin Books Ltd, 80 Strand, London WC2R ORL, England
Penguin Group (USA) Inc., 375 Hudson Street, New York, New York 10014, USA
Penguin Group (Canada), 90 Eglinton Avenue East, Suite 700, Toronto, Ontario, Canada M4P 2Y3
(a division of Pearson Penguin Canada Inc.)
Penguin Ireland, 25 St Stephen's Green, Dublin 2, Ireland (a division of Penguin Books Ltd)
Penguin Group (Australia), 707 Collins Street, Melbourne, Victoria 3008, Australia
(a division of Pearson Australia Group Pty Ltd)
Penguin Books India Pvt Ltd, 11 Community Centre, Panchsheel Park, New Delhi – 110 017, India
Penguin Group (NZ), 67 Apollo Drive, Rosedale, Auckland 0632, New Zealand
(a division of Pearson New Zealand Ltd)
Penguin Books (South Africa) (Pty) Ltd, Block D, Rosebank Office Park, 181 Jan Smuts Avenue,
Parktown North, Gauteng 2193, South Africa

Penguin Books Ltd, Registered Offices: 80 Strand, London WC2R ORL, England

www.penguin.com

First published 2013
001

Typeface ArcherPro by Hoefler & Frere-Jones
Designed by Giulia Garbin
Colour Reproduction by Tag: response
Printed in China

A CIP catalogue record for this book is available from the British Library

ISBN: 978-0-241-14564-7

Penguin Books is committed to a sustainable
future for our business, our readers and our planet.
This book is made from Forest Stewardship
Council™ certified paper.

To my students, future, past and present

Contents

9 Introduction

15 A Note on Japanese Measurements

17 Glossary

19 Useful Equipment & Utensils

25 Sushi Rice

29 Hosomaki · Small Roll

37 Ura Hosomaki · Small Inside-out Roll

49 Futomaki · Giant Roll

59 Ura Futomaki · Giant Inside-out Roll

69 Bo Sushi

75 Temaki · Hand Roll

85 Temari Sushi · Hand-ball Sushi

95 Oshi Sushi · Pressed Sushi

103 Chirashi Sushi

111 Soba Sushi · Buckwheat Noodle Sushi

121 Inari Sushi

127 Sashimi

135 Koryori & Soup · Small Dishes & Soup

145 Preparing Fish & Seafood

153 Dashi · Japanese Stock

162 Stockists

163 Menu Plans

167 Acknowledgements

169 Index

Introduction

Sushi in Japan

When I was a child and my mother would say that we were going to have sushi tonight, I would be filled with excitement. I was excited about the food, of course, but also about where and how we would be eating it – would we be making it at home or going somewhere special? Sushi eaten at a restaurant and home-style sushi are quite different for Japanese people. Sushi is a unique food culture, a cuisine within a cuisine: anything from the blur of dishes as they pass in a kaiten (conveyor-belt) sushi restaurant; to super-fresh sliced nigiri, those beautiful slices of fish resting on a rice pillow, in a small restaurant next to Tsukiji fish market amongst the bustle of the market traders; to high-end Kyoto dining while watching geishas pass by; to the bento boxes you see hundreds of smartly dressed children taking to school every day.

My grandmother always took me to a fantastic traditional sushi restaurant. For me, the experience of eating sushi in this restaurant was completely different from cooking and eating it at home. When I walked in, I was greeted with different words from those used in other sorts of restaurants, and the quiet calm and the mesmerizing sight of the chef's flawless movements as he cut the fish made me feel immediately that I was somewhere special. It is this attention to detail, presentation, preparation and the enjoyment of the process that unites sushi in all its forms. When the Japanese salaryman rolls out his napkin, puts down his bento box and arranges his chopsticks to one side before beginning his lunch, it is the ceremony he has in mind, a chance to escape and enjoy something luxurious.

Japan has always had specialities – sushi restaurants, tempura restaurants, eel restaurants, and so on. The people who work there spend years honing their skills. Itamae master sushi chefs – and these are almost always men, rarely women – begin by working at sushi restaurants as apprentices when they are teenagers. Training takes years: they start by washing the rice, and it can be four years before they progress to washing the fish, let alone cutting it.

Although this may seem a strange and lengthy process, it demonstrates how much Japanese culture respects its food. Japanese people do not eat sushi every day, and it is often considered a meal for a special occasion. The array of Japanese restaurants serving ramen, katsu curry and yakitori in London alone is testament to the growing popularity and variety to be found within Japanese cooking.

Making Sushi at Home

I respect Japanese sushi culture, but as a woman from a younger generation who has studied in America and lived in the UK, I like to take a different approach: after all, with home cooking, you can't spend four years learning to wash rice. Thankfully, there's a difference between going out and respecting tradition, and making something lovely to eat at home.

With nigiri, you have to slice the fish very quickly, touching it only once – in fact, my old mentor doesn't use his right hand at all to touch the fish – and you would never make nigiri at home, because it wouldn't taste right. But you can make temari, which is very similar in style, easy to make, and looks stunning. If it's nigiri you are looking for, then save your appetite for the many high-end restaurants and enjoy watching the beautiful work of a master sushi chef!

So the ingredients, the setting and the atmosphere may change, but the general approach in all cases is a real care for the food's preparation and the quality of ingredients. Sushi always feels like a treat, a fine-dining experience, but it can be prepared easily at home. Sushi is a cuisine in itself, defined in all its forms by the pride taken in making something really special and delicious. Whatever the setting, sushi is my favourite food and I always delight in teaching people how to make it.

Sushi is not something to be afraid of. You need to learn a few methods to prepare beautiful sushi at home, but don't worry – this is not about spending ten years training in a Kyoto kitchen or using expensive equipment; in fact, I'll be showing you how to use a hairdryer to perfect your rice. And nowadays you can buy a huge range of Japanese products very easily, without breaking the bank.

The most important thing is keeping an open mind: whether you want to use caviar or cucumber, as long as you enjoy what you make, then that is fine.

A simple pasta dish is truly great if you use fresh, good-quality pasta cooked properly; similarly, if you make good rice, then you can make wonderful sushi. Japanese food is very simple to make, it is one of the healthiest ways to eat and it can be easily incorporated into your daily life. Achieving the equivalent of al dente perfection can be a precise process, so follow the methods carefully and enjoy the challenge. Get the basics right, be discerning with your ingredients and experiment!

My Approach

Japanese food is so delicious that it is easy to forget that it is healthy too, and I love teaching people how to prepare it. My approach is based on three principles:

Chisan, chisho – 'produce locally, eat locally'
As far as possible use ingredients that can be bought easily and locally: ready-cooked crab, smoked salmon, mackerel, asparagus, cucumber, avocado, spinach and green beans, for example. Of course, we don't live in a bubble, and Japanese food would be impossible to create without some key ingredients from further afield. Luckily, sushi rice, nori, wasabi and other formerly hard-to-find products are all now widely available in supermarkets and online, which makes it much easier, but my sushi recipes are designed to be accessible and enjoyed by anyone keen to learn, in any location.

Nowadays you can eat everything, everywhere, at any time. However, I recommend trying to use the ingredients available to you, as inventiveness improves the experience. It was only when my family visited Tokyo that we would eat Edomae, or Tokyo-style sushi, for example. I love exploring different parts of England at the weekend and using Norfolk smoked fish or Cornish crab to create new recipe combinations, and I grow some of the more difficult-to-find ingredients, like the herb shiso, in my garden.

Otaku – '[be a] geek!'
Talk to your grocer and your fishmonger. Care about the ingredients and the process. Be fussy about what you use in your dishes and where it comes from. There are no short cuts or tricks if you don't have good fresh fish or vegetables. When I first took my friends to Japan we caught the bus to Yamanashi, a

journey of two hours or so. The whole way there, three elderly but very lively ladies were having a passionate chat. Keen to know the subject, my friend was surprised to discover that they had been talking about food – in this case pickles – for over two hours: the best way to pickle daikon, its health benefits, its taste, what time of year to do it, the beautiful colours you could achieve depending on which vinegars were used, and so on.

Tejun and tegiwa – 'preparation and process'

Get the basics right. As with the example of al dente pasta, Japanese food is about getting some basic methods spot-on. To make perfect sushi rice, for example, it is critical to cool it down properly (not only to give it the right texture, but also for safety), and learning how to do this is integral to the process. It is really easy to do and makes all the difference. Skip it and it will not be right!

Fish and Sustainability

After freshness, local, sustainable and seasonal are the three points that I think are most important when buying food, and this applies when I am buying fish too. In my sushi classes, my students always ask about fish. Of course it is very important to find good-quality seafood, so when you find a good fishmonger, try to make friends with them. Don't be afraid to ask about the quality of the fish, its freshness and the recommended fish of the day.

It is very important to buy sushi- or sashimi-quality fish and seafood to make sushi or sashimi. Although there are no precise legal definitions of these terms, according to European Union guidelines sushi- or sashimi-quality fish and seafood has to be very fresh, taking note of possible food-borne illnesses from bacteria and parasites. So find a fishmonger that you trust. You don't have to go to a Japanese fishmonger – I go to good fishmongers on the high street.

Look out for the MSC logo on products. This certifies that the fish comes from a fishery that has been classed sustainable. All of the major supermarkets now stock MSC-certified fish and seafood, and you can also buy ethical, sustainable fish online – see 'Stockists', page 162, for details.

Try to use local fish such as mackerel and sea bream. Ask your fishmonger where and how the fish was caught. Look out for line-caught or pole-caught fish and hand-dived or creel-caught seafood, and avoid anything that has been bottom-trawled, beam-trawled or dredged in order to catch it. See 'Preparing Fish & Seafood', pages 145–51, for further information on freshness and sustainability.

Traditional Accompaniments to Sushi

Soy sauce and wasabi

In sushi restaurants in Japan it is usual for chefs to add the wasabi to the inside of the sushi before it is made – or, if you prefer, you can ask the chef to make the sushi without wasabi when your order is taken, which is what I did when I was a child. When you're making sushi at home, you can either add wasabi to the roll itself or, as I prefer to do, add it to the soy sauce and mix it with the end of your chopsticks, so that it combines – this way you can control the heat. Use as much wasabi as you like, although remember that you should be able to taste the sushi filling. Similarly, you should dip your sushi into the soy sauce or soy sauce and wasabi mixture gently, so that very little of it is absorbed: the sushi rice should not soak up lots of soy sauce. You are not making a risotto; it's an accompaniment, so don't drown the rice! If you're eating nigiri at a restaurant you should dip the edge of the fish, not the rice, into the sauce, otherwise it runs the risk of collapsing. If you're eating temari (a ball-shaped sushi that has thin layers of fish on top, but which can be made at home, unlike nigiri), then you should do the same. It's OK to use your hands, so don't worry if you haven't quite mastered your chopsticks yet.

Pickled ginger

Many people add a piece of pickled ginger to their sushi, which is fine, but it was originally intended as a palate cleanser. When you eat sushi – at a restaurant, or at home – you are often eating lots of different types of fish, and a small amount of pickled ginger in between each type of sushi helps to stop the different flavours becoming muddled.

There are no rules to serving sushi when you're cooking at home. If you were eating out, you might start with miso soup or sashimi – it's traditional for sushi bars to serve sashimi first, before you are too full – but at home you can serve dishes all together. If you are cooking for four people, say, I would make miso soup, one type of salad (one of the sashimi or seafood salads in this book) and three different types of sushi roll. Of course, it depends on the individual, but one hungry person will eat around twenty pieces. I like to mix everything up and serve different types of roll on a big platter. Contrary to what popular sushi chains would have us believe, in Japan you wouldn't arrange sushi pieces so that they sit flat on the plate, but would place them so that they are standing up, on their sides.

In Japan, green tea is served with sushi, but of course there's no reason why you shouldn't drink beer or wine – or, of course, sake.

Safety

Sushi vinegar helps to preserve sushi rice, but you should still consume it on the same day that it is made, and do not refrigerate it. I would recommend keeping sushi for no more than half a day once it is made.

A Note on Japanese Measurements

The traditional Japanese cup, called a gō, is equivalent to 180ml of liquid or 150g of rice. It is used throughout the book. Incidentally, a bottle of sake is normally 1.8 litres; we call this measurement a shou. Ten gō = one shou.

Rice Measurements
3 Japanese cups (450g) of rice make 1.1kg sushi rice
Small roll and small inside-out roll: 80g sushi rice = half a handful of sushi rice (can be 75–85g)
Giant roll and giant inside-out roll: 160g sushi rice = a handful of sushi rice (can be 160–170g)
Hand roll: 50g sushi rice = a small handful of sushi rice (can be up to 65g)
Bo sushi: 130g sushi rice
Temari sushi: 25g sushi rice
Inari sushi: 45g sushi rice

Glossary

abura-age: *thinly sliced and deep-fried tofu, used to make inari sushi*

aonori: *seaweed powder*

daikon: *Japanese radish; you can also use mooli*

dashi: *Japanese stock*

edamame: *boiled soya beans*

furikake: *a dry Japanese seasoning, sprinkled on to rice*

gari: *pickled ginger*

genmai miso: *brown rice* **miso**

hatcho miso: *blended with roasted barley, this is very dark brown and has a longer fermentation compared to other types of* **miso***. A unique and strong flavour*

hijiki: *sea vegetable, usually available dried and in small pieces*

ikura: *salmon roe (large roe)*

katsuobushi: *bonito flakes*

kinshi tamago: *Japanese-style egg crêpe*

kombu: *dried kelp, a sea vegetable with a very clear and gentle flavour available in sheet form or cut into pieces (usually 1cm x 3cm), normally used for making stock*

kombu dashi: *kelp stock*

kome miso: *rice-based* **miso***, blended with barley*

masago: *capelin roe (very small roe)*

mirin: *a Japanese sweet rice wine used for seasoning*

miso: *a paste produced by fermenting soya beans, rice and barley with salt and koji fungus, used to make soups or sauces. There are many different varieties of miso, like beer, and it is divided into dark (aka miso) or white (shiro miso); see* **genmai miso***;* **hatcho miso***;* **kome miso***;* **mugi miso***;* **saikyo miso**

mizuna leaves: *Japanese mustard greens*

mugi miso: *barley* **miso**

natto: *fermented soya bean*

nori: *seaweed sheet, mostly used for sushi*

panko: *Japanese breadcrumbs, slightly larger and rougher than the Western equivalent, are readily available in supermarkets in the specialist sections*

sake: *Japanese rice wine*

sesame seeds: *black seeds have a stronger, nuttier flavour than the white. Both are available at Asian and Arabic grocery*

saikyo miso: *blended with rice, this **miso** is very pale and has a shorter fermentation and lighter taste than other types. It originated in Kyoto and is gluten free*

shiso leaves: *Japanese herb (perilla leaves)*

soba noodles: *buckwheat noodles*

sushi rice: *cooked Japanese rice and **sushi-su***

sushi-su: *rice vinegar mixture*

tamari soy sauce: *darker and thicker than regular soy sauce. It is normally gluten-free and has a stronger flavour.*

tobiko: *flying-fish roe (small roe)*

tsuma: *shredded **daikon** normally used as a garnish for sashimi*

umeboshi: *Japanese pickled plum*

unagi: *freshwater eel, usually grilled with kabayaki sauce*

wakame: *sea vegetable, high in minerals, normally used for salad or soup and available dried and in small pieces. After soaking in water, these small soft leaves have a very subtle taste. It is a healthy emergency food, which can be easily kept in your store cupboard*

wasabi: *Japanese horseradish served with sushi or sashimi and used as an ingredient to add spiciness*

Useful Equipment
& Utensils

When you start cooking, it is helpful to learn good knife skills: not only will this give you more confidence, it will mean that you work more quickly and decrease the chance of injuring yourself!

Preparing fish and seafood can be a bit tricky, but remember that a good fishmonger will always be happy to prepare it for you, so don't worry if you are not confident about your cutting skills yet.

I am obsessed with knives. It is not necessary to choose an expensive one, but do try to find a good-quality knife which suits you. Always check the grip: it must feel comfortable and not too heavy. You can find Japanese knives in most kitchen shops or department stores; some are quite different in shape from Western knives, but you can use any knife as long as you feel comfortable with it. Here are some knives and other tools that might come in useful:

cling film: *use to keep sushi rice moist, to protect your sushi mat, and for making temari sushi; traditionally a muslin cloth would have been used*

fan: *very important for making sushi rice; you can use an electric fan, a traditional hand-held fan or the cool setting of a hairdryer*

Japanese knives: *these tend to be lighter, have little or no bolster and steely edges*

Bunka/Santoku knife: *a very common and general-purpose knife, which most Japanese people have in their kitchen*

Deba knife: *heavy and chunky-looking, this is used for sanmai-oroshi (boning and filleting fish)*

Yanagiba/sashimi knife: *this has a long and narrow shape and is used for slicing raw fish for sashimi or sushi*

Japanese omelette pan: *a rectangle-shaped pan, used for making dashi-maki tamago. Found in Japanese shops or online* oshi sushi kata (wooden oshi sushi box): *a mould for making oshi (pressed) sushi; a multi-size cake tin works as a good substitute – see 'Oshi Sushi', pages 95–7*

rice cooker: *very common in Japan, although I prefer using a non-stick pan*

strainers/sieves: *for washing rice and straining eggs*

suribachi: *a Japanese mortar*

surikogi: *a Japanese pestle*

sushi mat: *for rolling sushi; traditionally made from bamboo, though you can find modern silicon sushi mats. If using a bamboo mat, cover it tightly with cling film before you use it; it's a useful way to make the mat more hygienic, and easier to clean after rolling*

sushi oke: *a shallow wooden bowl used to mix cooked rice and sushi vinegar, for sushi rice; you can use a deep dish or roasting pan*

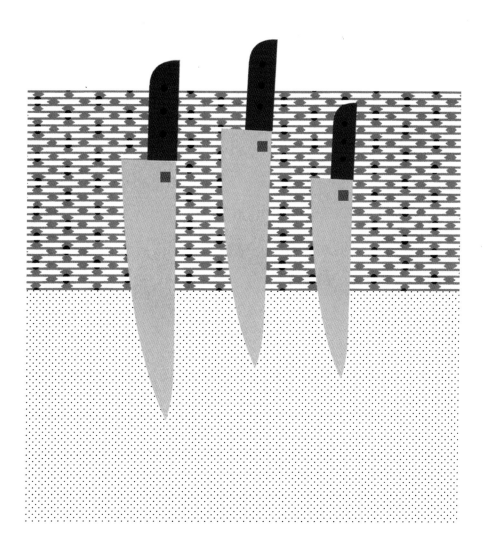

Recipes

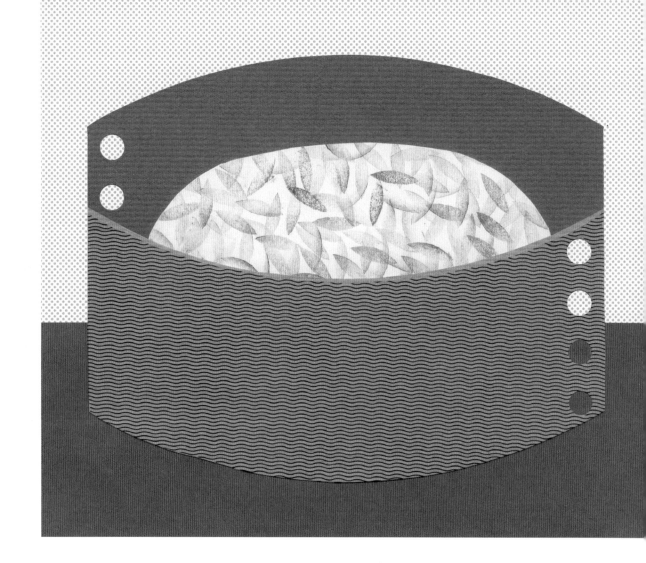

SUSHI RICE

酢飯

Rice is a staple in Japan. Just as Italian people are passionate about risotto – its consistency and how al dente it is, for example – Japanese people are mad about rice. When I go to a sushi restaurant with my family or friends, we talk about the rice quality as well as the quality of the fish.

We eat rice with every meal – and also, for a quick light meal or snack, in the form of rice balls, onigiri, or sprinkled with the Japanese seasoning furikake, or with pickles, just as other people eat buttered toast with jam or Marmite.

Japanese rice is short grain and sticky when cooked. For everyday meals, we usually eat white rice in which the bran part, nuka, has been polished away during the milling process, creating beautiful, shiny rice. We also eat brown rice, genmai, which has more fibre and is high in minerals. Traditionally, brown rice would not be used for sushi in Japan, but it's nice to have the option and it is becoming increasingly popular.

When making your own sushi, it is crucial that you use Japanese rice, which can easily be found in local supermarkets or Asian shops (see page 162 for stockists). You don't need any special equipment to cook it: you don't need a Japanese rice cooker, just a 20cm non-stick saucepan with a glass lid (you shouldn't open the lid when cooking rice). I use a large wooden bowl to make the rice, but you can use a deep dish or roasting pan. The most important thing is that it is fairly flat, so that the rice isn't layered too deeply.

SUSHI RICE
Su meshi or shari

This is my fail-safe method for preparing perfect rice. It is important to have a well-balanced rice vinegar mixture (sushi-su). My secret trick is using a fan or hairdryer to cool down the rice and prevent it from becoming too sticky.

Makes 1.1kg, enough for 13 small rolls or 7 giant rolls, to serve around 4 people

For the sushi-su (makes 125ml)
120ml rice vinegar or brown rice vinegar
3 tablespoons of sugar
1 tablespoon of sea salt

For the rice
3 Japanese cups (450g) of Japanese rice
3 Japanese cups (540ml) of water

To make the sushi-su, put the rice vinegar, sugar and salt into a pan and leave on a low heat until the sugar and salt have dissolved. Be careful not to let it boil or the flavour will spoil. Remove from the heat and leave to cool.

To make the rice, first wash it thoroughly in a sieve for 4 minutes, gently turning it over by hand until the water runs clear. Drain the rice and put it into a pan with the water. Leave it to stand for a minimum of 30 minutes. It can be left overnight, but for best results I recommend leaving it for 30 minutes to 1 hour.

Leaving the water in the pan, bring the rice to the boil, put the lid on and reduce the heat, letting it simmer for 8–9 minutes. Turn the heat off and let it stand with the lid on for a further 15 minutes. Do not open the lid.

Put the rice into a wide flat dish such as a sushi oke, a baking dish or a roasting pan. Pour the sushi-su over the rice and fold it carefully into the rice with a wooden spoon as it cools down, being careful not to damage the grains. You can use a fan or a hairdryer on the coolest setting to speed up the cooling process, directing it at the rice. The sushi-su gives the rice more flavour and that familiar sticky glazed look.

If you don't want to use the rice immediately, cover it with cling film or a damp cloth so that it doesn't dry out. Leave in a cool place, but do not refrigerate. The fridge will make the rice texture hard and dry, and the sushi-su helps to preserve the rice without refrigeration. It will keep for a day.

SUSHI BROWN RICE
玄米酢飯

Makes 1.1kg – enough for 13 small rolls or 7 giant rolls, to serve around 4 people

For the sushi-su (makes 125ml)
120ml rice vinegar or brown rice vinegar
3 tablespoons of sugar
1 tablespoon of sea salt

For the rice
3 Japanese cups (450g) of Japanese rice
5 Japanese cups (900ml) of water

To make the sushi-su, put the rice vinegar, sugar and salt into a pan and leave on a low heat until the sugar and salt have dissolved. Be careful not to let it boil or the flavour will spoil. Remove from the heat and leave to cool.

To make the Japanese brown rice, first wash it thoroughly in a sieve for 2 minutes, gently turning it over by hand until the water runs clear. Drain the rice and put it into a pan with the water. Leave it to stand for a minimum of 2 hours, or leave it overnight. It is very important that the rice soaks in the water for long enough as otherwise it can be undercooked in the centre. Brown rice has more fibre than white rice, so you need to soak and cook it for longer.

Leaving the water in the pan, bring the rice to the boil, put the lid on and reduce the heat, letting it simmer for 35 minutes. Turn the heat off and let it stand with the lid on for a further 15 minutes. Do not open the lid.

Put the rice into a wide flat dish such as a sushi oke, a baking dish or a roasting pan.

Pour the sushi-su over the rice and fold it carefully into the rice with a wooden spoon as it cools down, being careful not to damage the grains. You can use a fan or a hairdryer on the coolest setting to speed up the cooling process, directing it at the rice. The sushi-su gives the rice more flavour and that familiar sticky glazed look.

As in the recipe for sushi rice above, if you don't want to use the rice immediately, cover it with cling film or a damp cloth so that it doesn't dry out. Leave in a cool place, but do not refrigerate. It will keep for a day.

Tips
- Sushi-su will keep in the fridge for at least a few weeks, so I recommend that you make double the amount or more, but ensure you use the correct quantity for the amount of rice you are making.
- Use a non-stick pan for cooking the rice as it prevents it from burning and sticking to the bottom of the pan.
- Eat the sushi rice within a day. It is very important that the rice is fresh.

HOSOMAKI

Small Roll
細巻き

Hosomaki is a small sushi roll. In Japanese, *hoso* means an object that is small, petite or slim. It is a very traditional style of sushi and is familiar to many people. With its almost black nori seaweed sheet on the outside and the white rice on the inside, this roll looks very pretty. Just one filling, such as a thin stick of cucumber, raw fish or Japanese pickle is traditional, but you could also add a small amount of lettuce, or herbs such as shiso leaves, chives or basil. I usually cut them into 6 or 8 pieces. They are great for pre-dinner nibbles or canapés, and the layer of nori on the outside stops your fingers from getting sticky.

Tips

- Try a variety of fillings. I have described my favourite recipes here, but be inventive.
- It is not necessary to buy a Japanese knife, but do use your sharpest knife.
- When you make several rolls, roll everything first and then cover them with cling film or a damp tea towel until you are ready to cut them. They stay fresher this way. Do not keep them in the fridge as the rice will go hard.

KAPPA MAKI
Cucumber small roll
かっぱ巻き

Kappa maki is the most famous vegetable roll, with a simple filling of cucumber. The crunchiness of the cucumber is lovely, and usually I don't peel it as I love the texture with the skin on. Japanese cucumbers are slightly thinner than Western cucumbers, although they taste pretty much the same. When you buy a cucumber, try to choose one that is as straight as possible, as this will make it easier to roll.

Makes 4 rolls (24–32 pieces)
a sushi mat (if using a bamboo mat, cover it
   tightly with cling film)
a bowl of cold water for your hands
4 cucumber sticks, cut from a whole cucumber
   (see below)
2 sheets of nori
4 half-handfuls (roughly 320g) of sushi rice
2 teaspoons of toasted white sesame seeds,
   to serve

Slice the ends off a cucumber and cut it to the same length as the nori sheets (about 20cm). Cut it lengthways into 4 and remove the seeds carefully with a spoon or a knife. Cut the sticks lengthways into half again, so that you have 8 sticks of cucumber. You will need 4 sticks for this recipe, so wrap and store the rest in the fridge for 1–2 days to use in other sushi.

You will be able to see some thin lines on the nori seaweed sheets. Following one of these lines, cut each sheet in half with scissors, but be very careful as the sheets break easily. Place a half-sheet of nori shiny side down on the bottom half of the sushi mat, with the lines of the sheet lying horizontally across the mat.

Wet your fingers in the bowl of water, and shake off any excess. Damp fingers help when handling sticky sushi rice. Look for a line in the nori sheet about 1cm from the top. Keeping the top 1cm of the sheet clear, spread half a handful of rice (roughly 80g) over the sheet evenly and gently with your fingertips. Do not use too much rice and do not press it on to the sheet. It must be a very thin layer of rice.

Place the cucumber stick in the centre of the rice. You can add some wasabi to the centre of the rice before you add the cucumber, if you like.

To roll your sushi, follow the instructions below. Repeat with the remaining nori sheets and filling ingredients, then cut your rolls (see below).

Rolling the sushi
Holding the filling in place with your index fingers, start rolling with the mat from the bottom edge of the nori towards the top of the rice edge. Make sure both the rice and filling are held in place tightly. Open the mat. You should be able to see the 1cm piece of nori that does not have rice on it. Now finish rolling.

Cutting the sushi
Remove the sushi from the mat and place it on a clean, dry chopping board. Cut each roll into 6 pieces (or 8, if you would prefer very small pieces) with a sharp, wet knife. When

you cut the sushi, slice it very smoothly and quickly. I recommend wiping the knife clean after every cut.

Serving the sushi
Place the cucumber rolls on a plate and sprinkle with the toasted sesame seeds.

Tips
· These are great for taking on picnics, or to work or school in a bento box, as they keep fresh for longer than raw-fish fillings.
· You can buy ready-toasted sesame seeds, or heat a non-stick frying pan and dry-fry the sesame seeds for 3–5 minutes, shaking the pan until they turn golden brown and then letting them cool.

TEKKA MAKI
Tuna and wasabi small roll
鉄火巻き

Tekka maki is the most traditional small roll. It uses a lean part of tuna (akami) and wasabi. The word *tekka* means both 'iron' and 'fire', and there are different theories as to how this name came about. Some people believe that it refers to iron being heated in a fierce fire and turning red hot, as tekka rolls use lean tuna meat (red) and spicy wasabi (hot). But another theory comes from the name of gambling dens, called *tekkaba*. In the past Japanese people gambling in these dens would snack on this sushi, as it is very easy to eat with one hand while playing with the other. The name may therefore have arisen in this way, much like the etymology of 'sandwich' in the UK.

Makes 4 rolls (24–32 pieces)
a sushi mat (if using a bamboo mat, cover it tightly with cling film)
a bowl of cold water for your hands
180–200g fresh, sushi-quality tuna steak, 1cm thick (ask your fishmonger to prepare it for you)
2 sheets of nori
4 half-handfuls (roughly 320g) of sushi rice
fresh grated wasabi or wasabi paste

Slice the tuna lengthways into 1cm-wide strips. You should be able to get four 20cm-long strips from a 180–200g slice of tuna steak (although you may need to use a larger number of shorter strips, depending on the shape of your steak).

You will be able to see some thin lines on the nori seaweed sheets. Following one of these lines, cut each sheet in half with scissors, but be very careful as the sheets break easily. Place a half-sheet of nori shiny side down on the bottom half of the sushi mat, with the lines of the sheet lying horizontally across the mat.

Wet your fingers in the bowl of water, and shake off any excess. Damp fingers help when handling sticky sushi rice. Look for a line in the nori sheet about 1cm from the top. Keeping the top 1cm of the sheet clear, spread half a handful of rice (roughly 80g) over the sheet evenly and gently with your fingertips. Do not use too much rice and do not press it on to the sheet. It must be a very thin layer of rice.

After placing the sushi rice on the nori,

add the wasabi paste to the centre of the rice. You can use as much as you like, but be warned that it is very hot! Place a 20cm-long slice of tuna on the top of the wasabi paste.

To roll your sushi, follow the instructions on page 30. Repeat with the remaining nori sheets and filling ingredients, then cut each roll into 6–8 pieces (see pages 30–31).

Tip
• It might be wise to make these rolls without wasabi if they are for children.

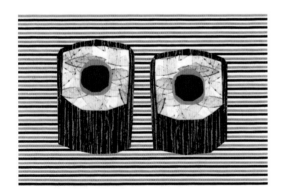

DAIKON OSHINKO MAKI
Pickled Japanese radish small roll
大根のお新香巻き

Japanese people are crazy not only about rice but pickles too. They are served with the main course or between courses, to cleanse the palate. A wide variety of pickles are made from local and seasonal ingredients such as different types of radishes, aubergine, cucumber or cabbage. Some vegetables are pickled for years in a mixture of malted rice, yeast, vinegar, spices, soy sauce, miso and salt. Many people use secret family recipes that are passed on from generation to generation.

Japanese pickles are delicious eaten alone with rice, almost like a version of the English cheese-and-pickle sandwich. Daikon, or Japanese radish, has a crunchy texture and unique flavour, making it perfect for pickling. Daikon oshinko (*oshinko* means 'pickled') is quick and simple to make, and good to have as a standby in the fridge. Make sure that you prepare it 24 hours before making your sushi. You can buy ready-pickled daikon if you don't have time to make it in advance.

Makes 4 rolls (24–32 pieces)
a sushi mat (if using a bamboo mat, cover it tightly with cling film)
a bowl of cold water for your hands
4 strips of daikon oshinko (see recipe opposite)
2 sheets of nori
4 half-handfuls (roughly 320g) of sushi rice

For the daikon oshinko
500g daikon (Japanese radish) or mooli
1 tablespoon of sea salt
80g brown sugar
90ml tamari soy sauce
40ml rice vinegar
1 dried red chilli
5cm x 5cm piece of dried kombu (kelp)

If you are making your own daikon oshinko, peel the daikon and cut it into 1cm-wide sticks the same length as the nori sheets (about 20cm). Sprinkle with the salt and leave for half an hour on a plate. Pat dry with paper towels. Put all the ingredients for the pickling sauce into a pot on a low heat until it begins to boil, and remove from the heat.

Place the daikon in a container and pour the hot sauce over it, leaving it to cool. Once the daikon mix is cool, keep it in the fridge for 24 hours before using. It can be kept in the fridge for a few weeks. When you use it for sushi, pat it dry with a paper towel so that you don't end up with a soggy roll.

You can now make your sushi. You will be able to see some thin lines on the nori seaweed sheets. Following one of these lines, cut each sheet in half with scissors, but be very careful as the sheets break easily. Place a half-sheet of nori shiny side down on the bottom half of the sushi mat, with the lines of the sheet lying horizontally across the mat.

Wet your fingers in the bowl of water, and shake off any excess. Damp fingers help when handling sticky sushi rice. Look for a line in the nori sheet about 1cm from the top. Keeping the top 1cm of the sheet clear, spread half a handful of rice (roughly 80g) over the

sheet evenly and gently with your fingertips. Do not use too much rice and do not press it into the sheet. It must be a very thin layer of rice.

Place the daikon in the centre of the rice. You can add some wasabi to the centre of the rice before you add the daikon, if you like.

To roll your sushi, follow the instructions on page 30. Repeat with the remaining nori sheets and filling ingredients, then cut each roll into 6–8 pieces (see pages 30–31).

Tips
- This pickling method also works well with cucumber or carrots.
- You could slice the daikon into even thinner slices, so that it will be ready to eat after just a night in the fridge. But if you want to use it as a sushi filling, you should cut it into 1cm-wide pieces, as these look better when the rolls are sliced.
- No need for extra soy sauce when serving, as pickled daikon has a strong soy flavour.

NATTO NEGI MAKI
Natto with chives small roll
納豆巻き

Natto is a fermented Japanese food made from soya beans. It has a strong, distinctive smell and a sticky, gooey texture. Fermented food like natto is, like Marmite, an acquired taste – but beware, it is famously addictive in spite of its strong smell! Japanese people eat natto with rice for breakfast. It is delicious mixed with mustard and soy sauce and is very popular as a sushi filling.

Makes 2 rolls (12–16 pieces)

a sushi mat (if using a bamboo mat, cover it tightly with cling film)
a bowl of cold water for your hands
5 strands of chives, chopped
2 half-handfuls (roughly 160g) of sushi rice
1 pack (50g) natto (without the soy sauce and mustard)
1 sheet of nori

Mix the chives with the sushi rice in a small bowl; the green chives and white sushi rice look great together. Roughly break up the natto with a knife.

You will be able to see some thin lines on the nori seaweed sheet. Following one of these lines, cut the sheet in half with scissors, but be very careful as it breaks easily. Place a half-sheet of nori shiny side down on the bottom half of the sushi mat, with the lines of the sheet lying horizontally across the mat.

Wet your fingers in the bowl of water, and shake off any excess. Damp fingers help when handling sticky sushi rice. Look for a line in the nori sheet about 1cm from the top.

Keeping the top 1cm of the sheet clear, spread half a handful of rice (roughly 80g) over the sheet evenly and gently with your fingertips. Do not use too much rice and do not press it on to the sheet. It must be a very thin layer of rice.

Place half the natto in the centre of the rice using a spoon, as it is very sticky and stringy.

To roll your sushi, follow the instructions on page 30. Repeat with the remaining nori sheet and filling ingredients, then cut your rolls into 6–8 pieces (see pages 30–31).

Tips
- Use different types of herbs such as shiso leaves, parsley or coriander, or even spring onion, instead of chives.
- Each pack of natto usually comes with Japanese mustard and soy sauce. I do not recommend adding these sauces when making sushi rolls as it will make the mixture too runny, but I love to mix the mustard and soy sauce in a bowl of plain rice.

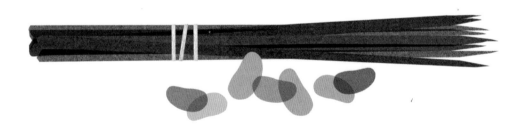

URA HOSOMAKI

Small Inside-out Roll
裏細巻き

Ura hosomaki is a small rice roll that has the rice on the outside and the seaweed on the inside. It was not eaten originally in Japan and is more popular in Western countries: the California roll (an inside-out roll typically filled with crabstick, avocado and cucumber) is the most famous sushi roll in America.

Ura hosomaki are good fun to make, and it's easy to create your own types of sushi. You can sprinkle jewel-like tobiko (flying-fish roe), white sesame seeds, black sesame seeds or aonori (powdered seaweed) on the outside of the rolls, all of which look very colourful and pretty, although you need to balance the flavours on the outside with the fillings. A roll with fresh salmon inside and tobiko on the outside is a perfect combination as there is a contrast between the soft texture of the salmon and the popping texture of the tobiko.

You roll with just one or two fillings, and I usually cut the rolls into 6 or 8 pieces.

Tips
- If the filling sticks out from the side of the rolls, don't feel that you have to trim it off. It looks pretty sticking out when placed on the plate.
- As always, use a very sharp knife. After cutting each slice I recommend cleaning your knife, especially as inside-out rolls are more difficult to slice because the rice on the outside sticks to the knife more easily.
- When you make several rolls, do not cut them into pieces until you need them. They stay fresher this way.

SIMPLE AVOCADO URA HOSOMAKI
Avocado with black sesame seeds
small inside-out roll
アボカドと黒ごまの裏細巻き

Avocado is not a traditional Japanese ingredient, but new generations of Japanese people love it as a sushi filling because the creamy, rich taste is like a vegetarian version of fatty tuna (toro). It is also a healthy option and goes well with any type of raw fish or shellfish – but I love simple avocado rolls with the addition of good-quality fresh wasabi. The most important thing is choosing perfect ripe and ready-to-eat avocados, so I usually buy a couple a few days before I plan to make sushi.

Makes 4 rolls (24 pieces)
a sushi mat (if using a bamboo mat, cover it
  tightly with cling film)
a bowl of cold water for your hands
1 large avocado
2 sheets of nori
4 half-handfuls (roughly 320g) of sushi rice
4 teaspoons of black sesame seeds

Cut the avocado in half lengthways around the stone. Twist and separate the two halves. Holding the half with the stone, tap the stone firmly and carefully with the sharp point of a knife blade and twist – the stone should lift out easily. Peel the skin neatly and slice the avocado lengthways into 1cm-wide crescent-shaped pieces.

You will be able to see some thin lines on the nori seaweed sheets. Following one of these lines, cut each sheet in half with scissors, but be very careful as the sheets break easily. Place a half-sheet of nori on the bottom half of the sushi mat, with the lines of the sheet lying horizontally across the mat; it does not matter if the shiny side is facing down or up because the nori won't be seen in the finished roll.

Wet your fingers in the bowl of water, and shake off any excess. Damp fingers help when handling sticky sushi rice. Look for a line in the nori sheet about 1cm from the bottom. Keeping the bottom 1cm of the sheet clear, spread half a handful of rice (roughly 80g) over the sheet evenly and gently with your fingertips. Do not use too much rice and do not press it on to the sheet. It must be a very thin layer of rice.

Sprinkle 1 teaspoon of black sesame seeds over the rice; these will end up on the outside of the roll. Hold the left side of the nori with both hands and flip it over on the mat, so that the nori is face up. Place a quarter of the avocado pieces at the bottom of the nori, on the area without rice. You can add some wasabi to the nori before you add the avocado, if you like.

To roll your sushi, follow the instructions below. Repeat with the remaining nori sheets and filling ingredients, then cut your rolls (see below).

Rolling the sushi
Holding the filling in place with your index fingers, start rolling with the mat from the bottom edge, little by little. Keep rolling 3 or 4 times, and each time you roll, open the mat and make sure that it is tightly rolled, so that there are no gaps between the filling and the

nori. Make sure both the rice and filling are held in place tightly every time you roll.

Cutting the sushi

Remove the sushi from the mat and place it on a clean, dry chopping board. Cut each roll into 6 pieces with a sharp, wet knife. When you cut the sushi, slice it smoothly and quickly. I recommend wiping the knife clean after every cut.

Tips

- Choose avocados which have shiny dark skins and make sure there is no visible damage. Buy an extra avocado, just in case!
- To ripen avocados perfectly, place them in a paper bag with a banana for a few days. The ethylene gas from the banana makes the avocados ripen.

SEA BREAM AND CORIANDER URA HOSOMAKI

Sea bream and coriander with white sesame seeds small inside-out roll
鯛とコリアンダーの裏細巻き

This is one of my signature dishes when I teach my sushi classes. It is easy to find sea bream in local fishmongers and coriander in supermarkets. The gentle taste of the sea bream and the exotic aroma of the coriander is a great combination.

Makes 4 rolls (24 pieces)

a sushi mat (if using a bamboo mat, cover it tightly with cling film)
a bowl of cold water for your hands
1 x 400g whole sea bream, or 2 fillets (150g each) of sea bream
2 sheets of nori
4 half-handfuls (roughly 320g) of sushi rice
4 teaspoons of white sesame seeds
a small bunch of coriander

If you are filleting a whole sea bream yourself, see page 149 for instructions. If you have bought fillets of sea bream, slice each fillet lengthways into 1cm-wide strips. You should be able to get four 20cm-long strips from two fillets (although you may need to use a larger number of shorter strips, depending on the shape of your fish).

You will be able to see some thin lines on the nori seaweed sheets. Following one of these lines, cut each sheet in half with scissors, but be very careful as the sheets break easily. Place a half-sheet of nori on the bottom half of the sushi mat, with the lines of the sheet lying horizontally across the mat; it does not matter if the shiny side is facing down or up because the nori won't be seen in the finished roll.

Wet your fingers in the bowl of water, and shake off any excess. Damp fingers help when handling sticky sushi rice. Look for a line in the nori sheet about 1cm from the bottom. Keeping the bottom 1cm of the sheet clear, spread half a handful of rice (roughly 80g) over the sheet evenly and gently with your fingertips. Do not use too much rice and do not press it on to the sheet. It must be a very thin layer of rice.

Sprinkle 1 teaspoon of white sesame seeds over the rice; these will end up on the outside

of the roll. Hold the left side of the nori with both hands and flip it over on the mat, so that the nori is face up. Place a 20cm-long strip of sea bream at the bottom of the nori, on the area without rice, and top with a quarter of the coriander. You can add some wasabi to the nori before you add the filling ingredients, if you like.

To roll your sushi, follow the instructions on pages 38–9. Repeat with the remaining nori sheets and filling ingredients, then cut each roll into 6 pieces (see page 39).

SHIME SABA AND SHISO URA HOSOMAKI

Marinated mackerel and shiso leaves with white sesame seeds small inside-out roll
しめ鯖としその葉　裏細巻き

One of my favourite recipes is shime saba, and I love shime saba sushi! *Shime* means 'cured fish', and *saba* means 'mackerel'. I cure the fish twice: first with sea salt, then with rice vinegar. The marinade gives the fish a pleasant acidic flavour that isn't overpowering and slightly 'cooks' it.

Shiso leaves look like nettle leaves but they have no sting and have a fresh, delicate flavour. You can find them in Japanese supermarkets or Asian shops, although I buy seeds from the Internet and grow them in my garden or in a pot on the windowsill during summer, just as you would with basil. If you can't find shiso then you can use coriander instead; it has a different aroma but both work very well with mackerel.

I usually fillet and prepare whole mackerel myself. To fillet mackerel the Japanese way – sanmai-oroshi: cut into three pieces, with two fillets and the backbone – see page 149.

Makes 4–6 rolls (24–36 pieces)
a sushi mat (if using a bamboo mat, cover it tightly with cling film)
a bowl of cold water for your hands
2 fillets of marinated mackerel (see recipe below)
2–3 sheets of nori
4–6 half-handfuls (roughly 320–480g) of sushi rice
4–6 teaspoons of white sesame seeds
6–9 shiso leaves, cut in half lengthways, or a small bunch of coriander (leaves only, or leaves and stems)

For the marinated mackerel
1 x 400–600g whole mackerel, or 2 fillets (100g each) of mackerel
2 big handfuls (60g) of sea salt
400–500ml rice vinegar or brown rice vinegar (or sufficient to cover the fillets)

If you are filleting the mackerel yourself, see the instructions on page 149. To marinate the mackerel, place the fillets on a flat plate, sprinkle the salt over each side of them and rub it in gently. Leave the fillets for an hour and then rinse them under running cold water and pat dry with a paper towel. For the final curing, place the fillets in a deeper dish, pour the rice vinegar over them until they are covered and leave for 45 minutes. Remove the mackerel from the vinegar and pat dry with a paper towel.

Pin-bone the fillets using tweezers to pull out the sturdy bones. When you run your finger over the surface of the fish, you can feel if there are any bones. They are usually found in the centre of the fillet. Then, starting at the corner of the fillet, peel off the skin using tweezers (see photos on pages 71–2).

You can now make the sushi. Slice the mackerel into short, 1cm-wide pieces. You should be able to get 6–10 slices from a single fillet.

You will be able to see some thin lines on the nori seaweed sheets. Following one of these lines, cut each sheet in half with scissors, but be very careful as the sheets break easily. Place a half-sheet of nori on the bottom half of the sushi mat, with the lines of the sheet lying horizontally across the mat; it does not matter if the shiny side is facing down or up because the nori won't be seen in the finished roll.

Wet your fingers in the bowl of water, and shake off any excess. Damp fingers help when handling sticky sushi rice. Look for a line in the nori sheet about 1cm from the bottom. Keeping the bottom 1cm of the sheet clear, spread half a handful of rice (roughly 80g) over the sheet evenly and gently with your fingertips. Do not use too much rice and do not press it on to the sheet. It must be a very thin layer of rice.

Sprinkle 1 teaspoon of white sesame seeds over the rice; these will end up on the outside of the roll. Hold the left side of the nori with both hands and flip it over on the mat, so that the nori is face up.

Place 3 shiso leaf-halves (or a third of the coriander) at the bottom of the nori, on the area without rice, and top with 3 marinated mackerel strips (or enough to lay along the bottom of the nori in a single strip, depending on the size of your fish). You can add some wasabi to the nori before you add the filling ingredients, if you like.

To roll your sushi, follow the instructions on pages 38–9. Repeat with the remaining nori sheets and filling ingredients, then cut each roll into 6 pieces (see page 39).

Tips

- Mackerel and other oily fish spoil more quickly than white fish, so I recommend buying as fresh a fish as possible from a high-quality fishmonger, who will also be able to fillet it for you.
- When you buy whole mackerel, check for clear, bright eyes as an indicator of freshness. The body has to be firm and shiny and the fish should not smell fishy.
- Marinate the mackerel on the day of purchase. After marinating it in the rice vinegar you will be able to keep it for three days in the fridge or freeze it for a few weeks. However, it is best eaten on the day.
- You can marinate it for up to 2 hours if you would like a stronger vinegary flavour and a slightly more 'cooked' appearance.
- Removing the fine layer of top skin using tweezers after marinating the mackerel leaves attractive markings on the fish.
- I recommend using a boning knife and a filleting knife if cutting the fish yourself.

UNA-Q AONORI URA HOSOMAKI

Grilled eel and cucumber with powdered
seaweed small inside-out roll
うなキュー裏細巻き

We refer to unagi (freshwater eel) as a
super-stamina fish, because it has a lot of
calories, a rich flavour and a high nutritional
value. Unagi are very long and thin, with
white flesh, and look the same as the eels you
see in the UK, although the way they are
served in Japan is very different from
English jellied eels. In Japan they are grilled
over charcoal (a technique called kabayaki)
and brushed with a special sauce (tare),
which is very similar to teriyaki sauce. You
would normally eat them at special unagi
restaurants or buy them ready-grilled at the
supermarket.

This recipe uses pre-cooked unagi, which
already has the sauce added and is available
in most Japanese or Asian supermarkets. If
you are not able to find unagi, you can use
herring fillets pan-fried with tare instead. The
rich flavours of both unagi and herring go
very well with fresh cucumber.

Makes 4–5 rolls (24–30 pieces)
a sushi mat (if using a bamboo mat, cover it
   tightly with cling film)
a bowl of cold water for your hands
1 packet (2 fillets) of grilled unagi, or 2 fillets of
   herring kabayaki (see recipe opposite)
4–5 cucumber sticks, cut from a whole
   cucumber (see page 46)
2–2½ sheets of nori
4–5 half-handfuls (roughly 320–400g) of sushi
   rice

2–3 teaspoons of aonori (powdered seaweed)

For the herring kabayaki
2 fillets of herring, skinned and boned (ask
   your fishmonger to do this for you, or see
   page 149)
1cm-long piece of ginger, grated
2 tablespoons of soy sauce
1 tablespoon of mirin
1 tablespoon of sake
plain flour for dusting
1 tablespoon of vegetable oil

For the kabayaki sauce (tare)
3 tablespoons of soy sauce
1 tablespoon of brown sugar
1 tablespoon of sake

Slice the grilled unagi fillets into 1cm-wide
strips. You should be able to get 4–5 strips
from each fillet, so 8–10 strips altogether. Use
1½–2 strips per roll.

If you are making herring kabayaki,
marinate the herring fillets with the grated
ginger, soy sauce, mirin and sake for 20
minutes, then drain, discard the marinade
and pat them dry with a paper towel and dust
with flour. Meanwhile, put all the ingredients
for the kabayaki sauce into a small bowl and
mix well. Heat a non-stick frying pan, pour in
the oil and cook the fish for 3 minutes on
each side. Remove the fish from the pan. If
the pan is very greasy after you have cooked
the fish, wipe it clean with paper towels, but
be careful because the pan and oil will be
very hot. Pour the sauce into the pan and
cook for approximately 30 seconds, then
remove from the heat, reducing the sauce

until it caramelizes (if you keep cooking on the heat it can burn and become bitter). Once it is caramelized, glaze the fish with it. Place the fish fillets on a plate and let them cool. Slice the herring fillets lengthways into 1cm-wide strips. As with the unagi, you should be able to get 4–5 strips from a single fillet.

Slice the ends off a cucumber and cut it to the same length as the nori sheets (about 20cm). Cut it lengthways into 4 and remove the seeds carefully with a spoon or a knife. Cut the sticks lengthways into half again, so that you have 8 sticks of cucumber. You will need 4–5 sticks for this recipe, so wrap and store the rest in the fridge for 1–2 days to use in other sushi.

You will be able to see some thin lines on the nori seaweed sheets. Following one of these lines, cut each sheet in half with scissors, but be very careful as the sheets break easily. Place a half-sheet of nori at the bottom of the sushi mat, with the lines of the sheet lying horizontally across the mat; it does not matter if the shiny side is facing down or up because the nori won't be seen in the finished roll.

Wet your fingers in the bowl of water, and shake off any excess. Damp fingers help when handling sticky sushi rice. Look for a line in the nori sheet about 1cm from the bottom. Keeping the bottom 1cm of the sheet clear, spread half a handful of rice (roughly 80g) over the sheet evenly and gently with your fingertips. Do not use too much rice and do not press it on to the sheet. It must be a very thin layer of rice.

Sprinkle 1 teaspoon of aonori over the rice; this will end up on the outside of the roll. Hold the left side of the nori with both hands and flip it over on the mat, so that the nori is face up. Place 1–2 unagi or herring strips in a line at the bottom of the nori, on the area without rice, with 1 cucumber stick alongside.

To roll your sushi, follow the instructions on pages 38–9. Repeat with the remaining nori sheets and filling ingredients, then cut each roll into 6 pieces (see page 39).

Tips

- Look for packets of grilled unagi in the freezer sections of Japanese or Asian supermarkets.
- Instead of herring you can also use fresh sardine fillets.

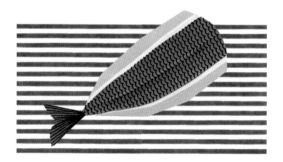

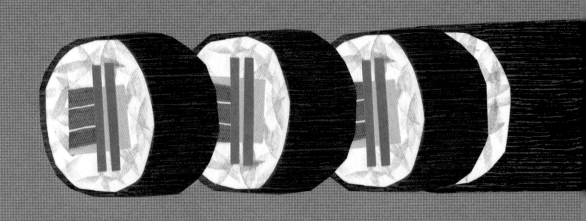

FUTOMAKI

Giant Roll
太巻き

Futo means 'fat', and these are giant rolls with the nori on the outside, using whole seaweed sheets. I usually put three different fillings into a futomaki, but they can be made with four or more. The technique is similar to making hosomaki. It might feel a little bit difficult to support all the fillings with your fingers when you start, but keep trying, as they are fun to roll! It is a good idea to use up leftover ingredients to make futomaki, and the different colours of the fillings make them very beautiful when sliced. I usually cut the rolls into 8–10 pieces.

Tips
- Try a variety of fillings.
- It is not necessary to buy a Japanese knife to make them, but do use a very sharp knife.
- When you make several rolls, roll everything first and cover them with cling film or a damp tea towel until you are ready to cut them. They stay fresher this way.

CLASSIC VEGETABLE FUTOMAKI
Dashi-maki tamago, braised shiitake mushrooms, carrots and cucumber giant roll
だし巻き卵,椎茸煮とキュウリの太巻き

This recipe is the most classic and authentic futomaki, and great for vegetarians. We refer to Japanese omelette as *gyoku* in sushi restaurants, and *dashi-maki tamago*, or *atsu-yaki tamago* (literally 'thick omelette'), at home. The dried shiitake-mushroom stock in the egg mixture gives it a great flavour and aroma, and keeps the omelette nice and moist. For the majority of Japanese cooking, you can use the kitchen equipment you already have, but you should invest in a Japanese omelette pan for this recipe, as the omelette must be square.

Shiitake mushrooms have a very strong flavour and are available in most local supermarkets. You will need 160ml of dried shiitake-mushroom stock, which is very quick and easy to make (see page 157). If you make the full 750ml recommended there, you can make a lovely miso soup with the remaining stock.

Makes 2 rolls (16–20 pieces)
a sushi mat (if using a bamboo mat, cover it tightly with cling film)
a bowl of cold water for your hands
1 x braised shiitake mushrooms and carrots (see recipe opposite)
1 x dashi-maki tamago (see recipe opposite)
2 cucumber sticks, cut from a whole cucumber (see page 51)
2 sheets of nori
2 handfuls (roughly 320g) of sushi rice

For the braised shiitake mushrooms and carrots
120ml dried shiitake-mushroom stock
4 shiitake mushrooms, from dried shiitake-mushroom stock
2 medium carrots, peeled
1 tablespoon of light or regular soy sauce
1 teaspoon of sugar

For the dashi-maki tamago (Japanese omelette)
Japanese rectangular omelette pan (11cm x 13cm)
2 large eggs
40ml dried shiitake-mushroom stock
¼ teaspoon of light soy sauce
a pinch of sea salt
½ teaspoon of caster sugar
1 tablespoon of oil for frying

First make the dried shiitake-mushroom stock, following the instructions on page 157, retaining 4 of the rehydrated mushrooms.

To make the braised shiitake mushrooms and carrots, slice the 4 rehydrated mushrooms very thinly and grate the carrots with the large side of a cheese grater. Put the sliced mushrooms, stock, grated carrots, soy sauce and sugar into a saucepan and bring to the boil, then reduce the heat and simmer for about 10 minutes until the vegetables are soft. Remove the pan from the heat and let it cool. Drain the juice if there is any excess.

To make the omelette, beat the eggs in a bowl and then add the other ingredients except the oil, mixing them well. Sieve the egg mixture into another bowl so that the mixture is smooth. Heat up the square frying pan until very hot and pour in the oil.

Carefully wipe the pan with a paper towel if the pan is too greasy. Pour a quarter of the egg mixture into the pan and let it cook until it starts to solidify, then fold it in half and half again so that it is a quarter of its size and is folded at the end of the pan. Add another quarter of the egg mixture and keep doing the same thing until all the egg mixture is used up and you have a firm block of omelette (11–13cm x 4–5cm size). Let it cool and cut into 4 long pieces.

To make the cucumber sticks, slice the ends off a cucumber and cut it to the same length as the nori sheets (about 20cm). Cut it lengthways into 4 and remove the seeds carefully with a spoon or a knife. Cut the sticks lengthways into half again, so that you have 8 sticks of cucumber. You will need 2 sticks for this recipe, so wrap and store the rest in the fridge for 1–2 days to use in other sushi.

You can now make the sushi. You will be able to see some thin lines on the nori seaweed sheets. Place a whole sheet shiny side down at the bottom of the sushi mat, with the lines of the sheet lying horizontally across the mat.

Wet your fingers in the bowl of water, and shake off any excess. Damp fingers help when handling sticky sushi rice. Look for the 2nd line from the top of the nori sheet, about 3–4cm down. Keeping the top 3–4cm of the sheet clear, spread a handful of rice (roughly 160g) over the sheet evenly and gently with your fingertips. Do not use too much rice and do not press it on to the sheet. It must be a very thin layer of rice.

Place 1 stick of cucumber, 2 pieces of omelette and half of the braised mushroom and carrot mixture side by side in the centre of the rice, along the length of the nori.

To roll your sushi, follow the instructions below. Repeat with the remaining nori sheet and filling ingredients, then cut your rolls (see below).

Rolling the sushi
Holding the fillings in place with your index, middle and ring fingers, start rolling with the

mat from the bottom edge of the nori towards the top of the rice edge. You might be nervous to start with, but just do it quickly, making sure both the rice and fillings are held in place tightly. Then open the mat. You should be able to see the 3–4cm piece of nori without rice on it. Now finish rolling – you may only need to use your hands for this, not the mat.

Cutting the sushi

Remove the sushi from the mat and place it on a clean, dry chopping board. Cut each roll into 8 or 10 pieces with a sharp, wet knife. When you cut the sushi, slice it very smoothly and quickly. I recommend wiping the knife clean after every cut.

Tips

- If the shiitake mushrooms are taking too long to soften when soaking, adding a pinch of sugar can help.
- Leftover Japanese omelette is very popular for bento boxes in Japan: just slice it into little cubes.
- It's nice to make a bright yellow omelette. I recommend buying eggs with orange or darker yolks, such as Old Cotswold Legbar hen eggs.

CLASSIC SEAFOOD FUTOMAKI

Salmon, crabmeat, avocado
and chives giant roll
海鮮太巻き

This recipe uses similar ingredients to a California roll. Salmon is one of my favourite fish, especially beautiful Scottish or Alaskan salmon. Chives have a great aroma and avocado gives a rich flavour: a lovely combination.

Makes 2 rolls (16–20 pieces)
a sushi mat (if using a bamboo mat, cover it
  tightly with cling film)
a bowl of cold water for your hands
80–100g fresh, sashimi-quality salmon fillet,
  1cm thick, skinned and boned (ask your
  fishmonger to do this for you)
1 avocado
a bunch of chives
2 sheets of nori
2 handfuls (roughly 320g) of sushi rice
150g white crabmeat

Slice the salmon lengthways into 1cm-wide strips. You should be able to get 2 x 20cm-long strips from an 80–100g slice of salmon (although you may need to use a larger number of shorter strips, depending on the shape of the fish).

Cut the avocado in half lengthways around the stone. Twist and separate the two halves. Holding the half with the stone, tap the stone firmly and carefully with the sharp point of a knife blade and twist – the stone should lift out easily. Peel the skin neatly and slice the avocado lengthways into ½cm–wide

crescent-shaped pieces. Wash the chives and leave the strands whole.

You will be able to see some thin lines on the nori seaweed sheets. Place a whole sheet shiny side down at the bottom of the sushi mat, with the lines of the sheet lying horizontally across the mat.

54

Wet your fingers in the bowl of water, and shake off any excess. Damp fingers help when handling sticky sushi rice. Look for the 2nd line from the top of the nori sheet, about 3–4cm down. Keeping the top 3–4cm of the sheet clear, spread a handful of rice (roughly 160g) over the sheet evenly and gently with your fingertips. Do not use too much rice and do not press it on to the sheet. It must be a very thin layer of rice.

Place half the salmon, half the chives, half the crabmeat and half the avocado side by side, in the centre of the rice, along the length of the nori. You can add some wasabi to the rice before you add the other ingredients, if you like.

To roll your sushi, follow the instructions on pages 51–2. Repeat with the remaining nori sheet and filling ingredients, then cut each roll into 8–10 pieces (see page 52).

Tips

- Buy the crab cooked and picked from your fishmonger, or see pages 150–51 if you would prefer to prepare it yourself.
- You could also use tinned crabmeat, and chopped spring onion instead of chives. But be sparing with the spring onions, as they are stronger.
- Use a perfectly ripe avocado.

KAKIAGE FUTOMAKI

Mixed vegetable and prawn tempura giant roll
かき揚げ太巻き

Kakiage is a variety of tempura which is very popular as a topping for udon or soba noodles. It is made from thinly sliced vegetables mixed with batter – very similar to the more well-known onion bhaji, although kakiage does not contain any Indian spices and uses plain flour instead of chickpea flour. I love to use prawns and a mixture of colourful vegetables such as red pepper, green pepper, celery and carrots.
I also add aonori (seaweed powder) to the batter, which makes the tempura look really pretty and gives a hint of seaweed aroma.

Makes 2 rolls (16–20 pieces)
a sushi mat (if using a bamboo mat, cover it
  tightly with cling film)
a bowl of cold water for your hands
2 sheets of nori
2 handfuls (roughly 320g) of sushi rice
4 kakiage tempura (see recipe below)

For the kakiage tempura
¼ of a red onion
½ a red pepper
½ a green pepper
4cm-long piece of carrot
½ a celery stalk
80g small raw prawns, peeled, tails removed
1 egg
220ml very cold water
80g sifted plain flour
1 tablespoon of aonori

plain flour for dusting
750ml–1 litre of vegetable oil for deep-frying

To make the kakiage tempura, slice all the vegetables lengthways into very thin strips. You could use a mandolin if you have one. Clean the prawns and pat dry with paper towels.

To make the batter, beat the egg and mix with the cold water. Pour the sifted flour and aonori into the water and egg mixture little by little, mixing it gently with chopsticks. Do not use a whisk or over-mix or the batter won't be fluffy and light. Dust the vegetables and prawns with flour, put them into the batter and mix together lightly.

Heat the oil in a deep frying pan or a deep fat fryer to 200°C. Remove a quarter of the prawn and vegetable mixture from the bowl with a big spoon and slide it gently into the oil, trying not to drop it. Do not touch it until it sticks together in the oil. After a few minutes, turn it over with chopsticks. It should take 3–4 minutes to cook, depending on the size of the tempura. Make sure it is cooked through but not overcooked. Remove from the oil, drain and place on paper towels to cool down. Repeat to make 4 tempura.

You can now make the sushi. You will be able to see some thin lines on the nori seaweed sheets. Place a whole sheet shiny side down at the bottom of the sushi mat, with the lines of the sheet lying horizontally across the mat.

Wet your fingers in the bowl of water, and shake off any excess. Damp fingers help when handling sticky sushi rice. Look for the 2nd line from the top of the nori sheet, about

3–4cm down. Keeping the top 3–4cm of the sheet clear, spread a handful of rice (roughly 160g) over the sheet evenly and gently with your fingertips. Do not use too much rice and do not press it on to the sheet. It must be a very thin layer of rice.

Place two pieces of kakiage tempura in the centre of the rice, along the length of the nori. You can add some wasabi to the centre of the rice before you add the tempura, if you like.

To roll your sushi, follow the instructions on pages 51–2. Repeat with the remaining nori sheet and filling ingredients, then cut each roll into 8–10 pieces (see page 52).

Tips

- For great vegetarian rolls, leave out the prawns and increase the amount of vegetables.
- For beautiful, crispy, light tempura, always keep the batter very cold – refrigerate it if necessary.

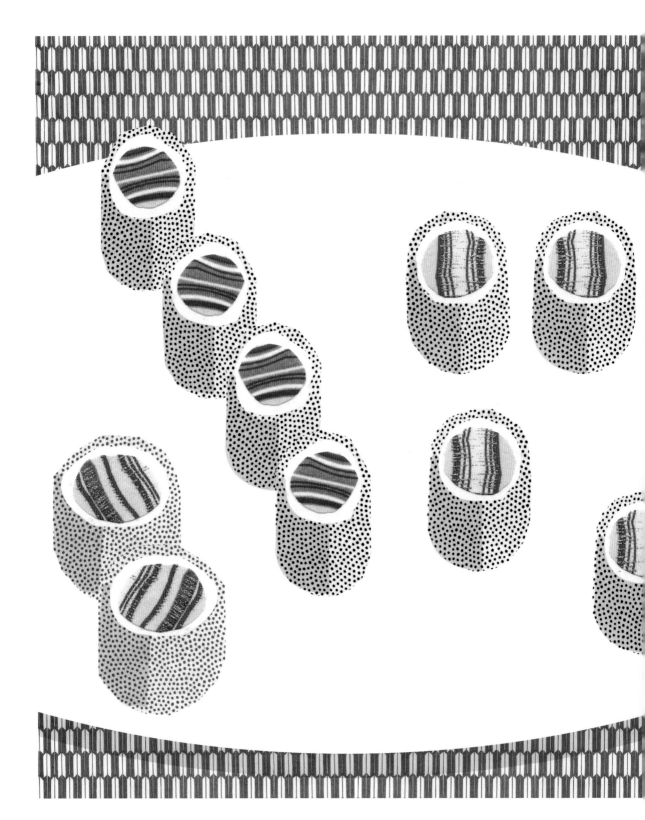

URA FUTOMAKI

Giant Inside-out Roll
太巻き

A more modern roll than classic futomaki, this combines the rolling techniques from the inside-out rolls and giant rolls. You might find it a little difficult to slice each piece because the rice is on the outside, so make sure your knife is sharp and clean every time you slice the sushi. I usually cut the rolls into 8–10 pieces.

Tips
- Try a variety of fillings and ingredients for the outside of the sushi: black sesame seeds, white sesame seeds, aonori and tobiko, for example.
- It is not necessary to buy a Japanese knife, but do use a very sharp knife.
- Wipe the rice off the knife after you cut each slice of sushi. Keep the knife clean and damp – it makes it much easier to slice the rolls.
- When you make several rolls, roll everything first and cover them with cling film or a damp tea towel until you are ready to cut them. They stay fresher this way.

KAISEN URA FUTOMAKI
Tuna, salmon and avocado
with tobiko giant inside-out roll
海鮮裏太巻き

These look very pretty, with the contrast of
the tuna and salmon next to the avocado and
the red roe on the outside, and taste clean
and fresh. You can choose any type of
sushi-quality tuna for this recipe. Akami, or
the lean part of tuna, is readily available and
balances the salmon and avocado well.

Makes 2 rolls (16–20 pieces)
a sushi mat (if using a bamboo mat, cover it
   tightly with cling film)
a bowl of cold water for your hands
80–100g fresh, sashimi-quality salmon fillet,
   1cm thick, skinned and boned (ask your
   fishmonger to do this for you)
80–100g fresh, sashimi-quality tuna steak, 1cm
   thick (ask your fishmonger to prepare it for
   you)
1 avocado, ripe but firm
2 sheets of nori
2 handfuls (roughly 320g) of sushi rice
2 tablespoons of tobiko (flying-fish roe) or
   masago (capelin roe)

Slice the salmon lengthways into 1cm-wide
strips. You should be able to get 2 x 20cm-
long strips from an 80–100g slice of salmon
(although you may need to use a larger
number of shorter strips, depending on the
shape of the fish). Repeat with the tuna steak.
   Cut the avocado in half lengthways
around the stone. Twist and separate the two
halves. Holding the half with the stone, tap

the stone firmly and carefully with the sharp
point of a knife blade and twist – the stone
should lift out easily. Peel the skin neatly and
slice the avocado lengthways into 1cm-wide
crescent-shaped pieces.
   Place a whole sheet of nori at the bottom of
the sushi mat, with the lines of the sheet lying
horizontally across the mat; it does not matter
if the shiny side is facing down or up because
the nori won't be seen in the finished roll.
   Wet your fingers in the bowl of water, and
shake off any excess. Damp fingers help
when handling sticky sushi rice. Look for the
2nd line from the bottom of the nori sheet,
about 3–4cm up. Keeping the bottom 3–4cm
of the sheet clear, spread a handful of rice
(roughly 160g) over the nori sheet evenly and
gently with your fingertips. Do not use too
much rice and do not press it on to the sheet.
It must be a very thin layer of rice.
   Sprinkle 1 tablespoon of tobiko or masago
over the rice; this will end up on the outside
of the roll. Hold the left side of the nori with
both hands and flip it over on the mat, so that
the nori is face up. Place half the tuna in a
single line at the bottom of the nori, on the
area without rice, then half the avocado strips
alongside, followed by half the salmon. It
should all fit on to the clear area of nori just
below the rice. You can add some wasabi to
the nori before you add the filling
ingredients, if you like.
   To roll your sushi, follow the rolling
instructions below. Repeat with the
remaining nori sheet and filling ingredients,
then cut your rolls (see below).

Rolling the sushi

Holding the fillings in place with your index fingers, start rolling with the mat from the bottom edge of the nori towards the top of the rice edge. Keep rolling 3 or 4 times, and each time you roll, open the mat and make sure that it is tightly rolled, so that there are no gaps between the fillings and the nori.

Cutting the sushi

Remove the sushi from the mat and place it on a clean, dry chopping board. Cut each roll into 8–10 pieces with a sharp, wet knife. When you cut the sushi, slice it very smoothly and quickly. I recommend wiping the knife clean after every cut.

Tip

- You can use any type of small fish roe. I love the texture of tobiko and richer flavour of masago.

UNAGI TAMAGO CUCUMBER URA FUTOMAKI

Eel, dashi-maki tamago and cucumber with
white sesame seeds giant inside-out roll
うなぎ、卵とキュリの裏太巻き

As this is a giant roll I like to add an extra
filling. Unagi (freshwater eel) does not go
with raw fish because the flavour of the unagi
would overpower it, but Japanese omelette is
a great match and it makes the roll look very
pretty. If you cannot find pre-cooked unagi
(which already has the sauce on it and is
available in most Japanese and Asian
supermarkets), you can use herring kabayaki
(see the recipe on page 45).

Makes 2 rolls (16–20 pieces)
a sushi mat (if using a bamboo mat, cover it
  tightly with cling film)
a bowl of cold water for your hands
½ a packet (1 fillet) of grilled unagi, or 1 fillet
  of herring kabayaki
2 cucumber sticks, cut from a whole
  cucumber (see below)
2 sheets of nori
2 handfuls (roughly 320g) of sushi rice
4 teaspoons of white sesame seeds
4 pieces of Japanese omelette (see recipe on
  page 50)

Slice the unagi or herring kabayaki fillet
lengthways into 1cm-wide strips. You should
be able to get 4–5 strips from 1 fillet, so 1–2
strips per sushi roll. To make cucumber
sticks, slice the ends off a cucumber and cut
it to the same length as the nori sheets (about
20cm). Cut it lengthways into 4 and remove

the seeds carefully with a spoon or a knife.
Cut the sticks lengthways into half again, so
that you have 8 sticks of cucumber. You will
need 2 sticks for this recipe, so wrap and
store the rest in the fridge for 1–2 days to use
in other sushi.

Place a whole sheet of nori at the bottom of
the sushi mat, with the lines of the sheet lying
horizontally across the mat; it does not matter
if the shiny side is facing down or up because
the nori won't be seen in the finished roll.

Wet your fingers in the bowl of water, and
shake off any excess. Damp fingers help
when handling sticky sushi rice. Look for the
2nd line from the bottom of the nori sheet,
about 3–4cm up. Keeping the bottom 3–4cm
of the sheet clear, spread a handful of rice
(roughly 160g) over the sheet evenly and
gently with your fingertips. Do not use too
much rice and do not press it on to the sheet.
It must be a very thin layer of rice.

Sprinkle 2 tablespoons of white sesame
seeds over the rice; these will end up on the
outside of the roll. Hold the left side of the
nori with both hands and flip it over on the
mat, so that the nori is face up. Place half the
unagi or herring strips in a single line at the
bottom of the nori, on the area without rice,
then 1 stick of cucumber alongside, followed
by 2 slices of omelette. It should all fit on to
the clear area of nori just below the rice.

To roll your sushi, follow the instructions
on page 61. Repeat with the remaining nori
sheet and ingredients, then cut each roll into
8–10 pieces (see page 61).

TUNA SALAD URA FUTOMAKI

Poached tuna wasabi mayo,
cucumber and mizuna with black
sesame seeds giant inside-out roll
ツナマヨサラダ裏太巻

A lot of people see sushi as just rice and raw fish, but I often describe it as the Japanese equivalent of the sandwich. When I was a child my mother would make sushi for my school lunch box and picnics, but she did not use raw fish. It is very common to use cooked fish or seafood for sushi fillings (especially when cooking for children), and I love tuna-mayo rolls. They fill me with nostalgia for my mother's cooking and are very popular in Japan, where you can find sushi made from cooked tuna and mayonnaise at takeaway sushi restaurants and convenience stores.

It may sound strange, but mayonnaise is very popular in Japan. Japanese mayonnaise usually has a slightly acidic taste and is stronger than regular mayonnaise as it is made using rice vinegar. You can use your favourite brand of mayonnaise or make your own. I use regular Western mayonnaise mixed with Japanese ingredients. Japanese tuna mayonnaise goes brilliantly with cucumber and mizuna. Mizuna is a green salad plant, with a peppery taste similar to rocket.

Makes 2 rolls (16–20 pieces)
a sushi mat (if using a bamboo mat, cover it
*   tightly with cling film)*
a bowl of cold water for your hands
200g fresh, sashimi-quality tuna steak, or
200g tinned or jarred tuna in spring water
2 cucumber sticks, cut from a whole
*   cucumber (see below)*
a handful of mizuna leaves or rocket leaves
2 sheets of nori
2 handfuls (roughly 320g) of sushi rice
2 tablespoons of black sesame seeds

For the wasabi mayonnaise
2 tablespoons of mayonnaise
1 teaspoon of wasabi paste
1 teaspoon of rice vinegar
a pinch of sea salt

If you are using fresh tuna, slice it into 1cm-wide pieces. Bring a saucepan with plenty of water to the boil and poach the tuna slices for a few minutes, then drain it well and pat it dry with paper towels. Leave to cool down. If you are using tinned or jarred tuna, make sure it is drained well.

Put all the wasabi mayonnaise ingredients into a bowl and mix well. Use your fingers to flake the tuna, and mix it into the wasabi mayonnaise.

Slice the ends off a cucumber and cut it to the same length as the nori sheets (about 20cm). Cut it lengthways into 4 and remove the seeds carefully with a spoon or a knife. Cut the sticks lengthways into half again, so that you have 8 sticks of cucumber. You will need 2 sticks for this recipe, so wrap and store the rest in the fridge for 1–2 days to use in other sushi.

Wash the mizuna or rocket leaves and dry well. Cut into the same length as the nori sheets.

Place a whole sheet of nori at the bottom

of the sushi mat, with the lines of the sheet lying horizontally across the mat; it does not matter if the shiny side is facing down or up because the nori won't be seen in the finished roll.

Wet your fingers in the bowl of water, and shake off any excess. Damp fingers help when handling sticky sushi rice. Look for the 2nd line from the bottom of the nori sheet, about 3–4cm up. Keeping the bottom 3–4cm of the sheet clear, spread a handful of rice (roughly 160g) over the sheet evenly and gently with your fingertips. Do not use too much rice and do not press it on to the sheet. It must be a very thin layer of rice.

Sprinkle 1 tablespoon of black sesame seeds over the rice; these will end up on the outside of the roll. Hold the left side of the nori with both hands and flip it over on the mat, so that the nori is face up. Place half the tuna wasabi mayonnaise in a single line at the bottom of the nori, on the area without rice, then 1 stick of cucumber alongside, followed by half a handful of mizuna or rocket leaves. It should all fit on to the clear area of nori just below the rice. You can add some wasabi to the nori before you add the filling ingredients, if you like.

To roll your sushi, follow the instructions on page 61. Repeat with the remaining nori sheet and ingredients, then cut each roll into 8–10 pieces (see page 61).

Tips
- If you cannot find mizuna or rocket, you can use other green salad leaves.
- You can buy Japanese mayonnaise at Japanese supermarkets. It already contains rice vinegar, so simply add the wasabi paste and salt.
- Children may not like wasabi, so use it with caution.
- Leftover sashimi- or sushi-quality tuna is great when poached the next day.

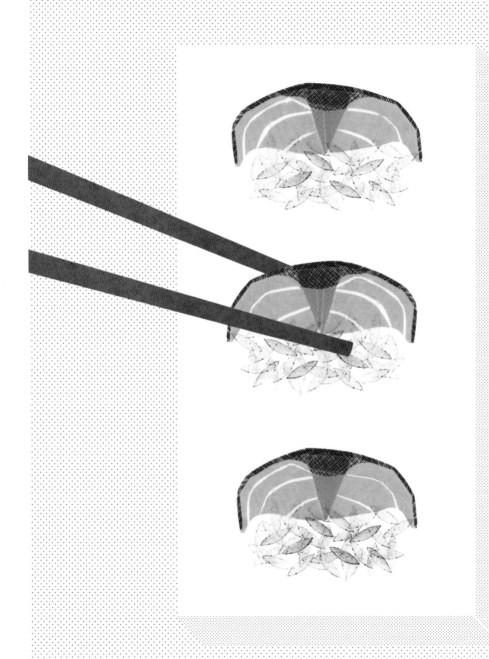

BO SUSHI

鯖棒寿司

Bo sushi is a very famous, authentic type of sushi, originally from the mid-west of Honshu. It is well known in the Kyoto region, where it is called 'saba [mackerel] sushi'. It is usually made using grilled fillet of mackerel, shime saba (marinated mackerel, see recipe on page 42) or unagi (freshwater eel). *Bo* means 'bar shape'; this is achieved by using cling film and a sushi mat to make long rectangles. Cut into 5–6 pieces, depending on the size of the mackerel.

Tips
- It is not necessary to buy a Japanese knife, but do use a very sharp knife.
- Keep the sushi tightly wrapped in cling film and do not cut until just before serving.

YAKI SABA BO SUSHI
Grilled mackerel bo sushi
鯖棒寿司

I love using grilled mackerel for this sushi, in the typical Japanese home-cooking style. If you cannot find fresh, sushi-quality mackerel from your fishmonger, you can use fish from a supermarket. I use pickled ginger, shiso leaves and white sesame seeds mixed with the sushi rice.

Makes 2 bo sushi (10–12 pieces)
a sushi mat (if using a bamboo mat, cover it
  tightly with cling film)
cling film
2 fillets of mackerel
260g sushi rice
2 teaspoons of finely chopped pickled ginger
3 shiso leaves or a small bunch of coriander
  leaves, finely chopped
2 teaspoons of toasted white sesame seeds

Place the mackerel fillets skin side up on a baking tray. Grill for 7–10 minutes under a medium-high heat until the skin is crispy and golden brown, then leave to cool down. If they are greasy, pat with kitchen paper to get rid of any excess oil. You can leave the skin on or, if you prefer, remove it gently and trim the fillets to make them a regular shape. Put the sushi rice into a bowl and mix with the pickled ginger, shiso leaves and sesame seeds.

Cut a sheet of cling film to roughly the same size as the sushi mat. Place the cling film on the mat and put a mackerel fillet in the middle. Spread half the sushi rice (130g) along the length of the mackerel.

Hold the bottom of the cling film with both hands and fold it over the top of the sushi rice. Fold the other side over the top to cover it tightly. Then use the sushi mat to form the roll into a long rectangle. Make sure the mackerel and rice are rolled tightly and stick together. Leave to rest for 5–10 minutes, and repeat with the remaining ingredients.

Cutting bo sushi
Place the bo sushi on a clean, dry chopping board. Trim the ends if you want and cut each bo sushi into 5–6 pieces through the cling film, using a sharp, wet knife. When you cut the sushi, slice it very smoothly and quickly. I recommend wiping the knife clean after every cut. Remove the cling film from each piece.

Tip
- Use pre-cooked unagi (freshwater eel, available from Japanese or Asian supermarkets), shime saba (marinated mackerel – see recipe on page 42) or smoked salmon instead of the mackerel.

SHIME SABA BO SUSHI
Marinated mackerel bo sushi
しめ鯖棒寿司

A beautifully shiny mackerel roll. Removing the top layer of skin with tweezers leaves some of the fish's pattern, which looks pretty.

Makes 2 bo sushi (10–12 pieces)
a sushi mat (if using a bamboo mat, cover it
*   tightly with cling film)*
cling film
260g sushi rice
2 teaspoons of toasted white sesame seeds
3 strands of chives, finely chopped
2 fillets of shime saba (marinated mackerel –
*   see recipe on page 42)*

If you are filleting the mackerel yourself, see the instructions on page 149. To marinate the mackerel, place the fillets on a flat plate, sprinkle the salt over each side of them and rub it in gently. Leave the fillets for an hour and then rinse them under running cold water and pat dry with a paper towel. For the final curing, place the fillets in a deeper dish, pour the rice vinegar over them until they are covered and leave for 45 minutes. Remove the mackerel from the vinegar and pat dry with a paper towel.

   Pin-bone the fillets using tweezers to pull out the sturdy bones. When you run your finger over the surface of the fish, you can feel if there are any bones. They are usually found in the centre of the fillet. Then, starting at the corner of the fillet, peel off the skin using tweezers.

Put the sushi rice into a bowl, add the sesame seeds and chopped chives and mix well.

Cut a sheet of cling film to roughly the same size as the sushi mat. Place the cling film on the mat and put a mackerel fillet in the middle. Spread half the sushi rice (130g) along the length of the mackerel.

Hold the bottom of the cling film with both hands and fold it over the top of the sushi rice. Fold the other side over the top to cover it tightly. Then use the sushi mat to form the roll into a long rectangle. Make sure the mackerel and rice are rolled tightly and stick together. Leave to rest for 5–10 minutes, and repeat with the remaining ingredients.

To cut your sushi, follow the instructions on page 70.

TEMAKI

Hand Roll
手巻き

Temaki, or hand roll, is cone-shaped and a very popular type of sushi. You often see it in takeaway shops, and it's also very simple and quick to make because you do not need to use a sushi mat or cutting techniques. It's fun and easy to have a hand-roll sushi dinner party with your family or friends. Just make the sushi rice, cut up the vegetables and fish and place everything on plates. You can use different kinds of salad leaves, cucumber, avocado, fresh or smoked salmon, tuna, and so on. Put it all on the table and let everyone make their own hand rolls. You just select the fillings, roll and eat!

Tips
- Try a variety of fillings.
- When placing the fillings on the rice, leave a little bit sticking out of the side of the nori sheet: it looks pretty when rolled up.
- Eat them immediately! The nori should be crunchy, not soggy.
- Serve them standing up in shot glasses as a fun snack.

UMEBOSHI AND CUCUMBER
WITH SHISO TEMAKI
Japanese pickled plum and cucumber
with shiso leaves hand roll
梅ときゅうり手巻き

Umeboshi are pickled plums, found in jars in
most Japanese homes. My grandparents had
an ume (plum) tree in their garden and made
their own pickles. I love to use umeboshi in
sushi as they have a very sour taste that
works well with other ingredients, such as
cucumber and aromatic shiso leaves. They
are also eaten with rice or as a side dish. As
with jam or chutney, everyone has their own
family recipes for umeboshi, but you can buy
them ready-made at Asian supermarkets and
some health-food shops.

Makes 4 rolls
a bowl of cold water for your hands
6cm-long piece of cucumber (see below)
4 teaspoons of ume paste, or 4 whole
    umeboshi (destoned)
2 sheets of nori
4 small handfuls (roughly 200g) of sushi rice
4 shiso leaves

Cut the piece of cucumber lengthways into 4
and remove the seeds carefully with a spoon
or a knife. Cut the sticks lengthways into half
again, so that you have 8 sticks of cucumber.
You will need 4 sticks for this recipe, so wrap
and store the rest in the fridge for 1–2 days to
use in other sushi. If you are using whole
umeboshi, mash them with the back of a
teaspoon.

You will be able to see some thin lines on
the nori seaweed sheets. Following one of
these lines, cut each sheet in half with
scissors, but be very careful as the sheets
break easily. Place a half-sheet of nori shiny
side down on your hand, with a short edge
closest to you.

Wet the fingers of your other hand in the bowl of water, and shake off any excess. Damp fingers help when using sticky sushi rice. Pick a small handful of rice (roughly 50g) and quickly spread it over the bottom half of the nori sheet. It does not have to be spread as neatly as the other types of rolls in this book. Place a shiso leaf diagonally in the middle of the rice, with an umeboshi and stick of cucumber on top.

Bring the bottom corner of the nori that is closest to you over the filling to meet the rice on the other side, making a triangle. You can then roll the plain side of the nori sheet around it to make a nice ice-cream-cone shape. (See photos on page 76.)

Repeat with the remaining nori sheets and filling ingredients.

Tip

- Umeboshi can have a very strong acidic and salty flavour, so you might not need to use soy sauce as a dip when you eat your roll.

EBI FURAI CHILLI-MAYO TEMAKI
Deep-fried prawn, Japanese panko breadcrumb and sweet chilli-mayo hand roll
海老フライ　チリマヨ手巻き

This is a very modern type of sushi and a popular Japanese home meal. *Ebi* means 'prawn' and *furai* means 'deep-fried'. Panko are Japanese breadcrumbs and are becoming very popular with many Western chefs, who use them for fried dishes. Panko crumbs are

slightly bigger and rougher than Western ones, which makes for a fluffier and lighter texture. I usually make my own panko: you can use leftover plain white bread and grate it with a food processor on the coarsest setting. You can also find ready-made panko crumbs in larger Western supermarkets.

Makes 4 rolls
a bowl of cold water for your hands
4 ebi furai (see below)
4 teaspoons of sweet chilli mayo (see recipe below), plus extra to serve
2 sheets of nori
4 small handfuls (roughly 200g) of sushi rice
4 tablespoons of cress

For the ebi furai
4 raw tiger or king prawns, shells on
a pinch of sea salt and pepper
plain flour for dusting prawns
1 egg, beaten
1 Japanese cup (roughly 40–50g) of panko (using 3 slices of white bread if you make your own)
750ml–1 litre of vegetable oil for deep-frying

For the sweet chilli mayo
2 tablespoons of Japanese mayonnaise; or 2 tablespoons of mayonnaise, ¼ teaspoon of English mustard and ½ teaspoon of rice vinegar
2 tablespoons of sweet chilli sauce
1 teaspoon of soy sauce

First prepare the ebi furai. Remove the heads and shells from the prawns. I like to leave the tails on because you can hold them when

dropping the prawns into the oil for deep-frying. De-vein the backs of the prawns with a skewer or toothpick. Clean the prawns under cold running water and pat dry with paper towels or a tea towel. Season with salt and pepper. Pull and stretch the prawns out gently to straighten them.

Put the plain flour, beaten egg and panko breadcrumbs into separate dishes. Dust the prawns with flour and dunk first in the beaten egg and then in the panko breadcrumbs. Leave them to rest for 5 minutes.

Heat the oil to 180°C in a deep frying pan or wok. Carefully add the prawns and fry them for 1 minute, then turn them over with chopsticks or tongs and fry for another minute until golden brown, but not overcooked. Remove them from the oil with a slotted spoon and place them on a paper towel to absorb the excess oil.

Put all the ingredients for the sweet chilli mayo into a small bowl and mix together well.

You can now make your sushi. You will be able to see some thin lines on the nori seaweed sheets. Following one of these lines, cut each sheet in half with scissors, but be very careful as the sheets break easily. Place a half-sheet of nori shiny side down on your hand, with a short edge closest to you.

Wet the fingers of your other hand in the bowl of water, and shake off any excess. Damp fingers help when handling sticky sushi rice. Pick up a small handful of rice (roughly 50g) and quickly spread it over the bottom half of the nori sheet. It does not have to be spread as neatly as the other types of rolls in this book. Place 1 teaspoon of sweet

chilli mayo diagonally in the middle of the rice, with 1 ebi furai and 1 tablespoon of cress on top. You can add some wasabi to the middle of the rice before you add the other ingredients, if you like.

Bring the bottom corner of the nori that is closest to you over the filling to meet the rice on the other side, making a triangle. You can then roll the plain side of the nori sheet around it to make a nice ice-cream-cone shape.

Repeat with the remaining nori sheets and filling ingredients. There will be some mayo left over, but you can add more to your roll!

Tip
• If you like spicier food, you can use chilli sauce instead of sweet chilli sauce.

SEA-BREAM CEVICHE TEMAKI
Japanese-style sea-bream ceviche hand roll
鯛セビーチェ手巻き

When I lived in the USA in the late 1990s, sushi was very fashionable and there were many fusion Japanese restaurants. I worked in a popular, modern Japanese restaurant in Chicago and learnt this recipe from a Peruvian colleague, who used to make a beautiful ceviche. The lime juice cooks the white fish and is very refreshing, making an amazing dish.

Peru and Japan have a great relationship as Peru was the first country in Latin America to have diplomatic relations with Japan and to accept Japanese immigrants.

Ninety thousand Japanese Peruvians now live in Peru and there are also large communities of Japanese in Brazil, so it seems fitting to use a mixture of South American and Japanese techniques to make this delicious sushi.

Makes 4 rolls
a bowl of cold water for your hands
2 fillets (150g each) of fresh, sushi-quality sea bream, skinned (ask your fishmonger to prepare it for you, or see page 149)
a pinch of sea salt
juice of 1 lime
1 shallot, chopped
a small handful of chopped coriander leaves
¼ teaspoon of wasabi paste
½ a red chilli, deseeded and finely sliced
a dash of light soy sauce
2 sheets of nori
4 small handfuls (roughly 200g) of sushi rice
8 strands of chives

Dice the sea-bream fillets into chunky pieces. They should not be diced too finely as you want them to retain their texture. Put the salt, lime juice, shallot, coriander, wasabi paste, red chilli and soy sauce into a small bowl, mix well and add the sea-bream chunks. Leave for an hour, or until the sea bream has turned milky-white in colour.

You will be able to see some thin lines on the nori seaweed sheets. Following one of these lines, cut each sheet in half with scissors, but be very careful as the sheets break easily. Place a half-sheet of nori shiny side down on your hand, with a short edge closest to you.

Wet the fingers of your other hand in the bowl of water, and shake off any excess. Damp fingers help when handling sticky sushi rice. Pick up a small handful of rice (roughly 50g) and quickly spread it over the bottom half of the nori sheet. It does not have to be spread as neatly as the other types of rolls in this book. Place a quarter of the ceviche mix diagonally in the middle of the rice, and place 2 strands of chives on top. You can add some wasabi to the middle of the rice before you add the other ingredients, if you like.

Bring the bottom corner of the nori that is closest to you over the filling to meet the rice on the other side, making a triangle. You can then roll the plain side of the nori sheet around it to make a nice ice-cream-cone shape.

Repeat with the remaining nori sheets and filling ingredients.

Tip
- You can use sea bass or any other white fish for this recipe, but it has to be very fresh, sushi-quality fish.

CREAMY SCALLOPS TOBIKO TEMAKI
Scallops and flying-fish roe with avocado sauce hand roll
帆立とアボカドソース手巻き

This is my favourite experimental recipe and a great starter! I love the richness and creaminess of the avocado and scallops.

Makes 4 rolls

a bowl of cold water for your hands

1-2 fresh, sushi-quality scallops (roughly 30g shelled weight in total)

½ a ripe avocado, destoned (see pages 60-61 on how to prepare)

a few drops of lemon juice

¼ teaspoon of wasabi paste

2 teaspoons of Japanese mayonnaise; or 1 tablespoon of mayonnaise, ¼ teaspoon of English mustard and ½ teaspoon of rice vinegar

a pinch of sea salt

1 tablespoon of tobiko (flying-fish roe), plus extra to garnish

2 sheets of nori

4 small handfuls (roughly 200g) of sushi rice

4 teaspoons of cress

Rinse the shelled scallops under cold running water and gently pat dry with paper towels. Slice them very thinly. Peel the avocado, put it into a small bowl and mash it with a fork until it is very smooth. Add the lemon juice, wasabi paste, mayonnaise and salt and mix well, to make the avocado sauce. Add the tobiko and scallops and mix gently.

You will be able to see some thin lines on the nori seaweed sheets. Following one of these lines, cut each sheet in half with scissors, but be very careful as the sheets break easily. Place a half-sheet of nori shiny side down on your hand, with a short edge closest to you.

Wet the fingers of your other hand in the bowl of water, and shake off any excess. Damp fingers help when handling sticky sushi rice. Pick up a small handful of rice (roughly 50g) and quickly spread it over the bottom half of the nori sheet. It does not have to be spread as neatly as the other types of rolls. Place a quarter of the scallop mix diagonally in the middle of the rice, and top with a teaspoon of cress. You can add some wasabi to the middle of the rice before you add the other ingredients, if you like.

Bring the bottom corner of the nori that is closest to you over the filling to meet the rice on the other side, making a triangle. You can then roll the plain side of the nori sheet around it to make a nice ice-cream-cone shape.

Repeat with the remaining nori sheets and filling ingredients.

Tips

- The scallops for this recipe must be very fresh. If you can find scallops in the shell, ask your fishmonger to remove them from their shells and clean them for you; or if you would like to shell them yourself, follow the instructions on page 151.
- You can use cooked prawns instead of scallops.
- You can use lumpfish roe or masago (capelin roe) instead of tobiko.
- If you are not using the other avocado half straight away, sprinkle lemon juice on the cut surface and wrap it tightly with cling film. It will keep in the fridge for 1-2 days.

TEMARI SUSHI

Hand-ball Sushi
手まり寿司

Temari is one of the easiest and quickest shapes for sushi. *Te* means 'hand' and *mari* means 'ball'. They are not only very easy to make but very colourful and pretty. You can use a variety of thinly sliced raw fish and I like to use smoked salmon as well.

Tip
- If you want to make temari for bento boxes, don't use raw fish, but try thin slices of Japanese omelette, cooked prawns, smoked salmon or avocado instead.

EBI TEMARI SUSHI
Prawn with lumpfish roe hand-ball sushi
エビとダンゴ魚キャビアの手まり寿司

You can use cooked prawns for this recipe if you do not want to cook them yourself. Lumpfish roe is a great garnish and adds a lovely flavour.

Makes 4 temari sushi
4 bamboo skewers
4 pieces of cling film (hand size)
a bowl of cold water for your hands
4 tiger or king prawns, raw or cooked, shells on
1 teaspoon of sea salt
1 half-handful (roughly 80g) of sushi rice
1 tablespoon of lumpfish roe

If using raw prawns, do not remove the heads and shells. Hold a prawn with one hand and, pointing a skewer away from the head of the prawn with the other, push the skewer between the shell and body towards the tail, making sure the prawn is straight. Repeat with the remaining prawns. Put plenty of water into a saucepan, add salt and bring to the boil, then add the prawns and cook for about 2–3 minutes. They will turn bright pink when they are done. Do not overcook them or they will be tough. Remove the prawns from the saucepan and quickly rinse them under cold running water. Drain, place them on paper towels and leave them to cool down completely. Once cool, remove the skewers.

Carefully peel the shells and heads from the cooked prawns, but leave the tails on. Butterfly the prawns by cutting open the belly side with a knife, being careful not to cut right through. Open the prawns up so that they are lying flat. You can then keep the tails on or remove them.

Place a sheet of cling film on the palm of your hand, and put a butterflied prawn on top. Wet the fingers of your other hand in the bowl of water, and shake off any excess. Damp fingers help when handling sticky sushi rice. Take a quarter of the sushi rice (roughly 20g) and place it on top of the fish. Bring the edges of the cling film into the centre, over the rice, and shape into a tight ball, then twist and close over the top. Unwrap the sushi and place on a plate. Repeat with the remaining ingredients.

Garnish with a ¼ tablespoon of lumpfish roe on top of each temari sushi.

Tip
· Make sure that the prawns are completely cool before removing the skewers. If they are still warm, they might curl up again.

OYAKO TEMARI SUSHI

Smoked salmon and salmon roe
hand-ball sushi
親子手まり寿司

One of the most popular Japanese street
foods is called *oyako don*, which means
'chicken and egg with rice in a bowl'. The
Japanese sense of humour has led to its also
being called 'mother and child', which
inspired me to call this recipe *oyako temari*:
the salmon being the mother, and the salmon
roe (ikura) the child. In spring, I like to make
a lot of oyako te mari and place it on a large
plate, to look like Japanese cherry blossom.

Makes 4 temari sushi
4 pieces of cling film (hand size)
a bowl of cold water for your hands
4 thin slices of smoked salmon, each roughly
  3–4cm square
1 half-handful (roughly 80g) of sushi rice
4 small pieces of dill
1 tablespoon of ikura (salmon roe)

Place a sheet of cling film on the palm of your
hand, and put a piece of smoked salmon on
top.

   Wet the fingers of your other hand in the
bowl of water, and shake off any excess.
Damp fingers help when handling sticky
sushi rice. Take a quarter of the sushi rice
(roughly 20g) and place it on top of the fish.
Bring the edges of the cling film into the
centre, over the rice, and shape into a tight
ball, then twist and close over the top.
Unwrap the sushi and place on a plate.
Repeat with the remaining ingredients.

Garnish with a piece of dill and 3–4 balls
of salmon roe on top of each temari sushi.

Tip
· You can use gravlax or good-quality raw
  salmon. You can also use tuna, but it won't
  be an oyako!

Makes 4 temari sushi

4 pieces of cling film (hand size)
a bowl of cold water for your hands
4 thin, sashimi-style slices of sea bream, each
  roughly 3–4cm square (see page 149 on how
  to prepare)
4 shiso leaves
1 half-handful (roughly 80g) of sushi rice
½ teaspoon of white sesame seeds

Place a sheet of cling film on the palm of
your hand, and put a piece of sea bream on
top, followed by a shiso leaf. After you have
rolled the ball, you will be able to see the
green colour of the leaf under the fish and
some at the sides.

Wet the fingers of your other hand in the
bowl of water, and shake off any excess.
Damp fingers help when handling sticky
sushi rice. Take a quarter of the sushi rice
(roughly 20g) and place it on top of the fish.
Bring the edges of the cling film into the
centre, over the rice, and shape into a tight
ball, then twist and close over the top.
Unwrap the sushi and place on a plate.
Repeat with the remaining ingredients.

Garnish with a small pinch of white
sesame seeds on top of each temari sushi.

SEA BREAM AND SHISO TEMARI

Sea bream and shiso hand-ball sushi
鯛としその手まり寿司

The paper-thin slices of sea bream allow you
to see the beautiful shiso leaves underneath.
Although this is a very simple recipe, it looks
stunning on the plate.

Tip

· The fish must be sushi- or sashimi-quality
  sea bream. Ask your fishmonger! You could
  also use sea bass.

HOTATE TEMARI SUSHI
Scallop and chives hand-ball sushi
帆立手まり寿司

If you don't want to remove scallops from
their shells yourself, you can buy them
already removed, or you can ask your
fishmonger to remove and clean them for
you, but do choose scallops that are as fresh
as possible. See page 151 for instructions on
how to shell scallops yourself.

Makes 4 temari sushi
4 pieces of cling film (hand size)
a bowl of cold water for your hands
*1–2 sushi-quality scallops (roughly 30g shelled
  weight in total)*
1 half-handful (roughly 80g) of sushi rice
½ tablespoon of chopped chives

Rinse the shelled scallops under cold
running water and gently pat dry with paper
towels. Slice each scallop very thinly into
wide slices. You should get 4 slices from a
scallop of around 30g.

Place a sheet of cling film on the palm of
your hand, and put a piece of scallop on top.
Wet the fingers of your other hand in the
bowl of water, and shake off any excess. Damp
fingers help when handling sticky sushi rice.
Take a quarter of the sushi rice (roughly 20g)
and place it on top of the fish. Bring the edges
of the cling film into the centre, over the rice,
and shape into a tight ball, then twist and
close over the top. Unwrap the sushi and
place on a plate. Repeat with the remaining
ingredients.

Garnish with chopped chives on top of
each temari sushi.

Tip
- When you buy scallops in their shells, store
  them round side down in the fridge, as that
  is how they naturally sit.

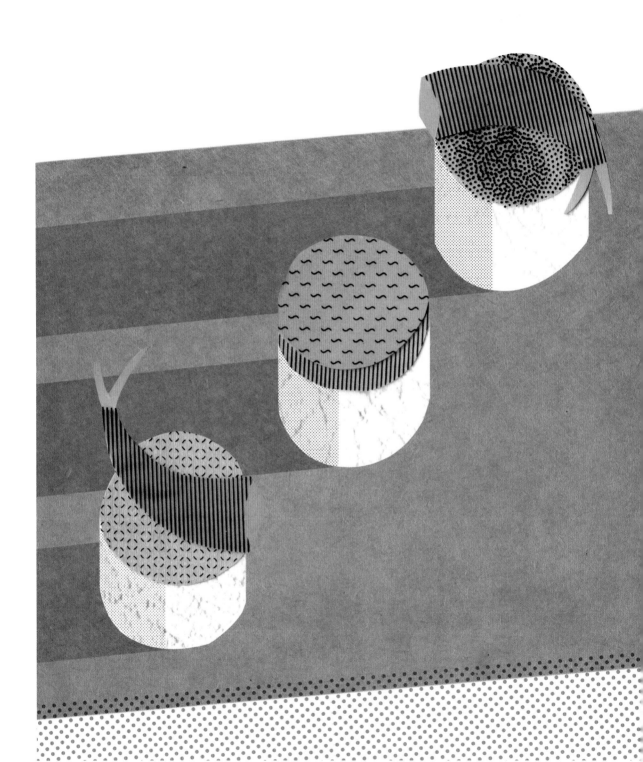

OSHI SUSHI

Pressed Sushi
押し寿司

Oshi means 'to press'. Traditionally oshi sushi is made using a wooden box, but you can also use cake tins, baking sheets, ramekins or even disposable juice cartons, to produce many different shapes. It is very easy to make and very pretty. You can serve it in individual portions or in larger sizes to share with your friends or family.

Tips
· Do not forget to line your mould with cling film!
· It is easier to slice the oshi sushi before removing the cling film.
· Wipe the knife clean after cutting every slice.

UNAGI AND AVOCADO OSHI SUSHI

*Japanese grilled eel and avocado
pressed sushi*
うなぎとアボカド　押し寿司

Pre-cooked unagi (grilled freshwater eel in kabayaki sauce) is often used for oshi sushi, as when pressed the kabayaki sauce mixes with the sushi rice. I like to accompany it with avocado so that you can see a green line in the middle of the sushi rice. I recommend using a traditional wooden oshi sushi box or a rectangular-shaped mould for this recipe, as grilled eel is long and narrow.

Makes 5–6 pieces

*7cm x 20cm x 5cm mould, or a multi-size
    adjustable cake tin
cling film, to line the mould
a bowl of cold water for your hands
½ an avocado, destoned (see pages 60–61 on
    how to prepare)
½ packet (1 fillet) of unagi, or 1 fillet of herring
    kabayaki (see recipe on pages 45–6)
2 handfuls (roughly 180g) of sushi rice
1 teaspoon of white sesame seeds, to garnish*

Line your mould with cling film, leaving enough cling film at the top to cover the sushi when it is made. Peel and slice the avocado very thinly. Cut the unagi or herring kabayaki to the same size as your wooden box or mould. Put half of the rice in the mould and place the avocado on top. Add the rest of the rice until the mould is three-quarters full.

Place the unagi or herring kabayaki on top of the rice and fold the cling film over the top. If the mould has a lid, press it firmly on top to compress the rice. If you do not have a lid, use a spoon or your fingers.

Carefully pull the oshi sushi out of the mould and slice it through the cling film into 5–6 pieces, or more if you wish. I like to cut it into small square pieces. Sprinkle with the sesame seeds and serve.

Tips

- You can make this a couple of hours in advance and slice it just before serving. Make sure you keep the sushi wrapped in cling film.
- You can use cucumber instead of avocado.
- If you are not using the other avocado half straight away, sprinkle lemon juice on the cut surface and wrap it tightly with cling film. It will keep in the fridge for 1–2 days.

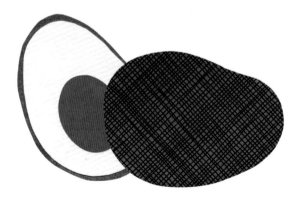

KANI AND EBI OSHI SUSHI
Crabmeat and king prawn mini pressed sushi
カニとエビのミニ押し寿司

This recipe is very popular with children, perhaps because it looks like a little cupcake. It uses cooked prawns and crab, so everyone loves it. I have had great fun decorating large versions for friends' birthday parties.

Makes 4 pieces
6cm-diameter mould or cake tin (a dariole mould or chef's ring can also be used)
cling film, to line the mould
280g sushi rice
100g cooked white crabmeat, or mixed white and brown crabmeat
4 cooked king prawns, peeled
1½ tablespoons of tobiko, capelin, ikura or lumpfish roe, to garnish
a few sprigs or leaves of herbs such as cress, dill, chives and coriander, to garnish

Line your mould with cling film, leaving enough cling film at the top to cover the sushi when it is made. Put a quarter of the rice in the mould. Add a quarter of the crabmeat, but be sure to keep 1cm free at the top.

Fold the cling film over the top. If the mould has a lid, press it firmly on top to compress the rice. If you do not have a lid, use a spoon or your fingers.

Carefully pull the oshi sushi out of the mould and remove the cling film. Place a prawn, a small amount of fish roe and a few pieces of cress or herb leaves on top, as a garnish. Repeat with the remaining ingredients.

Tips

- See pages 150–51 if you are preparing and cooking the crab yourself.
- Use a round mould roughly four times larger to make a version which looks like a big cake, multiplying the ingredients by four.
- You do not need to straighten the prawns for this recipe: the curved shape suits the round shape of the sushi.
- These pieces of sushi look lovely served on a cake stand.

MASU SUSHI
Trout with shiso leaves pressed sushi
鱒寿司

Masu means 'trout'. This oshi sushi is a very traditional regional food, originally from the Toyama prefecture in the mid-west of Japan. It is famously sold in bento boxes at stations, and is simple but very tasty. Traditionally, round wooden moulds are used, and the sushi is wrapped in bamboo leaves. It may be difficult to find bamboo leaves so I would recommend using cling film for this recipe.

Makes 6–8 pieces
20cm-diameter mould, or cake tin with
  removable base – a springform Victoria
  sponge tin works well
6–7 bamboo leaves or enough cling film to line
  the mould
700g sushi rice
6–8 shiso leaves
175–200g smoked trout, sliced very thinly

If using a cake tin, remove the base and place the tin on a flat, firm surface such as a chopping board. Line the inside of the mould or cake tin with the bamboo leaves or cling film, leaving enough of the leaves or cling film at the top to cover the sushi when it is made. Put half of the rice in the mould, to a depth of 2cm, place the shiso leaves on top of the rice, and then put the rest of the rice on top. Place the trout slices evenly on top of the rice.

Fold and tuck the bamboo leaves or cling film over the top, then put the lid of the mould or base of the cake tin on top and press hard. Place a weight on top (a full jam jar is ideal) and leave in a cool place for half an hour to set. You want it to become a little bit flat and to stick together. Carefully pull the oshi sushi out of the mould or tin, unwrap the leaves or clingfilm and slice the sushi into 6–8 pieces.

Tip
· You can use smoked salmon instead of smoked trout.

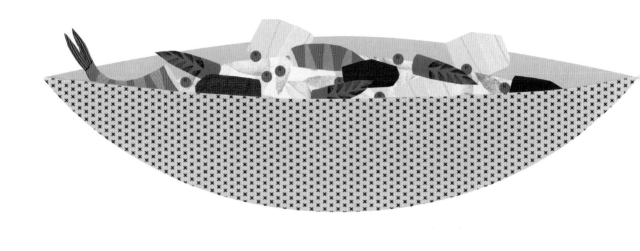

CHIRASHI SUSHI

ちらし寿司

Chirashi means 'to scatter', and this type of sushi consists of slices of fish, chopped fish or vegetables scattered on top of sushi rice. You do not need any special techniques for shaping the sushi, but each dish must have the right balance of taste and appearance.

You can serve chirashi on a large flat plate or a shallow bowl to share at the table, or in individual portions. I love to use lots of vegetables and colourful plates or bowls. Japanese lacquered wooden plates, called shitki or nurimono, look particularly lovely.

CLASSIC KAISEN CHIRASHI SUSHI

Seafood chirashi sushi

海鮮ちらし寿司

This recipe is a gourmet chirashi sushi. You can use your favourite fish and seafood, or whatever is available from the fishmonger. Sushi restaurants usually serve it in individual shallow bowls, and top the rice with generous slices of fish or seafood.

Serves 4

4 bamboo skewers
1 sheet of nori
400–600g sushi rice
1 tablespoon of white sesame seeds
2–4 fresh, sushi-quality scallops
4 king prawns, raw or cooked, shells on
1 teaspoon of sea salt
200g fresh, sushi-quality tuna steak
200g fresh, sushi-quality salmon, skinned and
*   boned (ask your fishmonger to do this for you)*
1 fillet of fresh, sushi-quality sea bream,
*   skinned (ask your fishmonger to do this for*
*   you, or see page 149)*
4 tablespoons of tobiko, masago, ikura or
*   lumpfish roe, to garnish*
1 tablespoon of cress, to garnish

Cut the nori into very thin strips (2mm x 20mm), using scissors. Place the sushi rice into 4 shallow bowls. Sprinkle the sesame seeds and nori on top of the rice.

If your scallops are small, slice them in half; if they are large, slice them into 4. If you have bought scallops in the shell and are preparing them yourself, see page 151.

If using raw prawns, do not remove the heads and shells. Hold a prawn with one hand and take a bamboo skewer in the other. Pointing the skewer away from the head of the prawn, push the skewer between the shell and body towards the tail, making sure the prawn is straight. Repeat with the remaining prawns. Put plenty of water into a saucepan, add salt and bring to the boil, then add the prawns and cook for about 2–3 minutes. They will turn bright pink when they are done. Do not overcook them or they will be tough. Remove the prawns from the saucepan and quickly rinse them under cold running water. Drain, place them on paper towels and leave them to cool down completely. Once cool, remove the skewers.

Carefully peel the shells and heads from the cooked prawns, but leave the tails on.

Place the tuna on a chopping board. Supporting it very gently with your fingers, slice it against the grain at a 20-degree angle into 8 pieces. Repeat with the salmon. Place the sea bream on the chopping board, and supporting it very gently with your fingers, slice it against the grain at a 20-degree angle into 16 very thin pieces.

Place all the prepared fish and seafood on the rice and nori. Garnish with the fish roe and cress, and serve with soy sauce and wasabi on the side.

HANA CHIRASHI SUSHI

Mixed seafood and vegetable chirashi sushi
華ちらし寿司

Hana means both 'flower' and 'gorgeous' in Japanese, so this sushi should look very pretty. The main difference between kaisen chirashi sushi and hana chirashi sushi is that the former uses large slices of fish, whereas the latter uses small pieces. It is best shared as a big plateful with friends or family.

Serves 4
600g sushi rice
2 tablespoons of toasted white sesame seeds
4 small asparagus spears
1 teaspoon of salt
4 mangetout
1 x dashi-maki tamago (see recipe on pages 50–51)
150g fresh, sushi-quality tuna steak, 1.5cm thick (ask your fishmonger to prepare it for you)
150g fresh, sushi-quality salmon fillet, 1.5cm thick, skinned and boned (ask your fishmonger to do this for you)
8 tiger or king prawns, raw or cooked, shells on
100g white crabmeat
4 teaspoons of ikura (salmon roe) and/or lumpfish roe, to garnish
a handful of cress, to garnish

Put the sushi rice and sesame seeds into a bowl and mix well. Place in a flattish pile in the middle of a large plate and leave to one side. Cut the asparagus spears into short pieces.

Add the salt to a saucepan of water and bring to the boil. Add the asparagus and cook for a minute, then add the mangetout. Cook for 1–2 minutes until the vegetables are tender but still firm. Do not overcook them! Immediately drain them and plunge them into a bowl of cold water. Drain again and slice the mangetout diagonally into thin julienne strips.

Cut the dashi-maki tamago, tuna and salmon into 1.5cm cubes.

If you are using raw prawns, follow the cooking instructions on page 104. Carefully peel the shells and heads from the cooked prawns, but leave the tails on.

Arrange the vegetables, dashi-maki tamago, tuna, salmon, prawns and crabmeat on top of the rice, so that the colours contrast prettily with each other. Garnish with the roe and cress.

Tips
- You can buy fresh crabmeat from the supermarket or your fishmonger, and tinned crab also works well in this dish. If you are preparing and cooking the crab yourself, see pages 150–51.
- You can use a variety of fish and seafood in this recipe, and lobster is great as a treat.

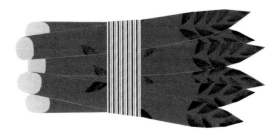

UNA-Q CHIRASHI SUSHI

Japanese grilled eel and cucumber
chirashi sushi
うなぎときゅうりのちらし寿司

This recipe uses cucumber marinated with sushi-su (sushi vinegar). The vinegary cucumber and slightly softer texture work well with chirashi sushi, and the individual flavours of the shiso-flavoured rice, unagi (freshwater eel), kinshi tamago (egg crêpe) and marinated cucumber all really stand out. It's a good idea to make this and una-q aonori ura hosomaki (see pages 45–6) at the same time as you need many of the same ingredients.

Serves 4
4 shiso leaves
600g sushi rice
5cm-long piece of cucumber
a pinch of sea salt
80ml sushi-su (see recipe on page 26)
½ a packet (1 fillet) of grilled unagi, or 1 fillet
  of herring kabayaki (see recipe on pages
  45–6)
1 large egg
a few drops of vegetable oil

Slice the shiso leaves very thinly and mix them well with the sushi rice in a bowl. Cut the piece of cucumber lengthways into half and remove the seeds with a spoon or a knife. Slice the cucumber very thinly into half-moon shapes and place in a bowl. Sprinkle a pinch of salt over and leave for 10 minutes, then squeeze the excess water from the cucumber. Place back into the bowl and mix with the sushi-su. After about 15 minutes, squeeze the excess vinegar from the cucumber.

Cut the unagi fillet or herring kabayaki into 1cm cubes.

To make the kinshi tamago, beat the egg very well in a small bowl. Put a small, non-stick frying pan over a medium heat and pour a few drops of vegetable oil into the pan. Carefully wipe the pan with a paper towel to remove any excess oil. Add the beaten egg and cook for 30 seconds, then flip the egg over and cook for a further 30 seconds. Make sure you do not overcook it. Remove the crêpe from the pan and leave it to cool down for 10 minutes, then cut it into very thin (2mm) slices. It should look like noodles.

Arrange the cucumber, unagi or herring kabayaki and kinshi tamago on the rice in an attractive way.

Tip
• Avocado also works really well instead of the cucumber.

HIJIKI CHIRASHI SUSHI

Braised sea vegetable
and shiitake mushrooms chirashi sushi
ひじきちらし寿司

Hijiki is a sea vegetable like wakame and kombu. It is rich in fibre and minerals – a delicious health food, with a unique flavour. It is becoming more popular in Western countries and therefore easier to buy at the supermarket. It is easy to store dried sea vegetables in the kitchen cupboard, and they are very useful when making salads or miso soup.

I do not use the recipe for sushi rice on page 26 in this recipe, as I prefer to use less sushi-su (sushi vinegar) because of the braised hijiki. The egg and edamame make a great colour contrast. This is the healthiest sushi ever!

Serves 4
2 Japanese cups (300g) of Japanese rice
2 Japanese cups (360ml) of water
50ml sushi-su (see recipe on page 26)
20g dried hijiki
1 large egg
a few drops of vegetable oil
1 teaspoon of sea salt
a half-handful (roughly 30g) of mangetout
1 handful (roughly 30g) of frozen podded edamame beans
1 medium carrot
100ml dried shiitake-mushroom stock (see recipe on page 157)
4 shiitake mushrooms, from dried shiitake-mushroom stock
2 tablespoons of soy sauce
1 tablespoon of mirin
1 tablespoon of sake
1 teaspoon of brown sugar

To prepare the rice, simply follow the method on page 26. Once prepared, put it to one side. Put the dried hijiki into cold water for 15–20 minutes, then rinse and drain them well and put this to one side too.

To make the kinshi tamago, beat the egg very well in a small bowl. Put a small, non-stick frying pan over a medium heat and pour a few drops of vegetable oil into the pan. Carefully wipe the pan with a paper towel to remove any excess oil. Add the beaten egg and cook for 30 seconds, then flip the egg over and cook for a further 30 seconds. Make sure you do not overcook it. Remove the crêpe from the pan and leave it to cool down for 10 minutes, then cut it into very thin (2mm) slices. It should look like noodles.

Add the salt to a saucepan of water and bring to the boil. Add the mangetout and edamame beans and cook for 2–3 minutes until the vegetables are tender but still firm. Do not overcook them! Immediately drain them and plunge them into a bowl of cold water. Drain again and slice the mangetout diagonally into thin julienne strips. Peel the carrot and cut lengthways into thin julienne strips, about 2mm x 15mm. Drain the shiitake mushrooms from the stock and slice them thinly.

Heat a tablespoon of oil in a non-stick frying pan and sauté the hijiki, shiitake mushrooms and carrot in the pan for a few minutes. Add the stock, soy sauce, mirin, sake and brown sugar, and simmer until the liquid has reduced (around 10 minutes), being careful not to let it burn. Mix the braised hijiki with the rice and serve on a flat plate, garnishing with the sliced mangetout and kinshi tamago on top.

Tips
- Leftovers are great in a bento box for lunch.
- You can buy edamame in their pods for this recipe, and pod them after cooking. Approximately 60g of pods will give you 30g of beans. The pods will take a little bit longer to cook, roughly 3–4 minutes.

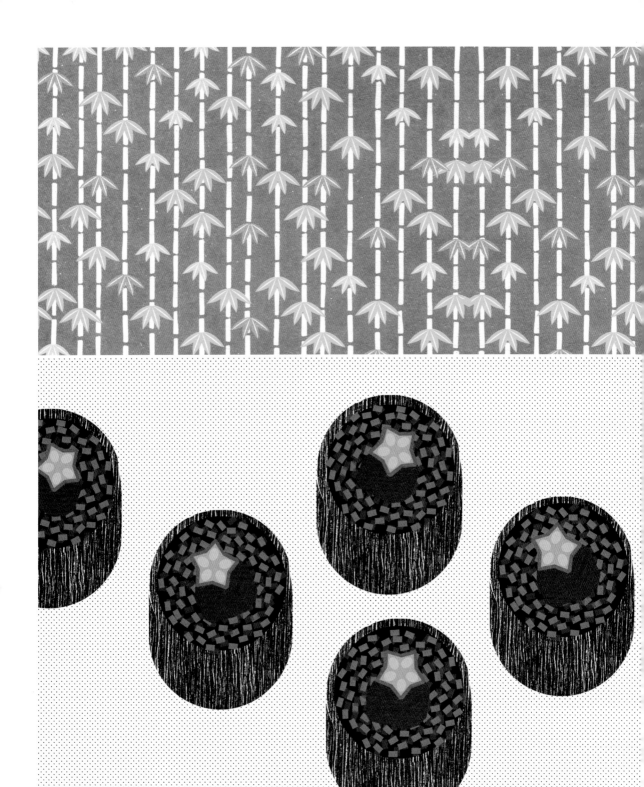

SOBA SUSHI

Buckwheat Noodle Sushi
蕎麦寿司

Soba is one of my favourite sorts of Japanese noodle. Made from buckwheat flour, these noodles have an earthy, beautiful taste and are usually served either cold, with a dipping sauce, or hot in a noodle soup. I was taught by the well-known master soba-noodle chef Mr Sekizawa, in Japan. He has a traditional soba-making room which is separate from the kitchen and is like a meditation room; he can focus on the art of making the fresh noodles here without any interruptions. He makes only 30–40 portions of fresh soba noodles every morning, using buckwheat flour which he orders directly from his chosen farm. His restaurant closes when he has sold out of noodles, sometimes as early as 1.30 p.m.

Buckwheat is gluten-free, and so you need to have a lot of experience to make pure soba noodles because it is very difficult to combine the ingredients together. Commercial soba noodles are usually blended with wheatflour to make them easier to produce and to reduce the cost. Luckily you can easily find dried soba noodles in Western supermarkets now. It's a good idea to keep a few packets in your cupboard.

Tip
· Experiment with different fillings, taking ideas from other recipes.

UNAGI, TAMAGO AND CUCUMBER SOBA SUSHI

Grilled eel, Japanese omelette and cucumber soba-noodle sushi

うなぎ、卵とキュウリの蕎麦寿司

Unagi (freshwater eel) is fantastic with soba noodles. I sometimes make unagi soba salad, which was the original inspiration for this sushi recipe. Be careful not to use too much of the tare sauce (which comes with the pre-cooked unagi) in the sushi, or it will become soggy.

Makes 2 rolls (16–20 pieces)
a sushi mat (if using a bamboo mat, cover it tightly with cling film)
½ a packet (1 fillet) of grilled unagi, or 1 fillet of herring kabayaki (see recipe on pages 45–6)
2 cucumber sticks, cut from a whole cucumber (see below)
120g dried soba noodles
1 teaspoon of vegetable oil
2 sheets of nori
1 x dashi-maki tamago (see recipe on pages 50–51)

Slice the grilled unagi or herring kabayaki into 1cm-wide strips. You should be able to get 4–5 strips from 1 fillet.

Slice the ends off a cucumber and cut it to the same length as the nori sheets (about 20cm). Cut it lengthways into 4 and remove the seeds with a spoon or a knife. Cut the sticks lengthways into half again, so that you have 8 sticks of cucumber. You will need 2 sticks for this recipe, so wrap and store the rest in the fridge for 1–2 days to use in other sushi.

Bring a large saucepan of water to the boil, add the noodles, and cook for 4–5 minutes. Every time the pan begins to foam, add a cup of cold water to prevent the foam from overflowing. The cold water helps to keep the noodles al dente. Drain them in a colander and rinse under cold running water. Drain again and toss with the vegetable oil to prevent the noodles from sticking. Pat them dry with a tea towel or paper towel.

Place a whole nori sheet shiny side down at the bottom of the sushi mat, with the lines of the sheet lying horizontally across the mat. Look for the 2nd line from the top of the nori sheet, about 3–4 cm down. Keeping the top 3–4 cm of the sheet clear, gradually place half the noodles in a very thin layer, horizontally, over the nori. Place a cucumber stick, half the unagi or herring and half the omelette side by side in the middle of the noodles, along the length of the nori. You can add some wasabi to the noodles before you add the other ingredients, if you like.

To roll your sushi, follow the instructions below. Repeat with the remaining nori sheet and filling ingredients, then cut your rolls (see below).

Rolling the sushi

Holding the fillings in place with your index, middle and ring fingers, start rolling with the mat from the bottom edge of the nori towards the top edge of the noodles. Try to do it quickly! Make sure the noodles and filling are held in place tightly. Then open the mat. You should be able to see the 3–4cm of nori that does not have noodles on it. Now finish rolling. Leave the rolled sushi in the sushi mat for 5 minutes so that the shape sets. It is not like sticky sushi rice, so it needs to be left for a while to set.

Cutting the sushi

Remove the sushi from the mat and place it on a clean, dry chopping board. Cut each roll into 8–10 pieces with a sharp, wet knife. When you cut the sushi, slice it very smoothly and quickly. I recommend wiping the knife clean after every cut.

EBI TEM CHA-SOBA SUSHI WITH UME-SU SAUCE

Prawn tempura and green-tea soba-noodle sushi with Japanese plum sauce

エビ天婦羅　茶蕎麦寿司

Cha means 'green tea'. These soba noodles are blended with green-tea powder – matcha – which gives them a beautiful colour and a sophisticated green-tea aroma. You can find them in Japanese or Asian shops, or online. If you are not able to find them, use regular soba noodles instead.

I like to use a simple prawn tempura for the filling, and serve it with a special dipping sauce instead of soy sauce. Japanese plum sauce is great, as the astringent flavour of the ume (plum) contrasts well with the rich, fried prawns.

Makes 2 rolls (16–20 pieces)
a sushi mat (if using a bamboo mat, cover it
    tightly with cling film)
4 prawn tempura (see recipe below)
120g dried green-tea soba noodles
1 teaspoon of vegetable oil
ume sauce (see recipe on page 114)
2 sheets of nori
4 tablespoons of cress

For the prawn tempura
4 raw tiger or king prawns, shells on
a pinch of sea salt and pepper
1 Japanese cup (180ml) of water, kept cold in
    the fridge
1 egg, kept cold in the fridge
80g plain flour, kept cold in the fridge
20g cornflour

1 teaspoon of baking powder
750ml–1 litre of vegetable oil for deep-frying

For the ume sauce
1 tablespoon of ume paste or a whole
  umeboshi (destoned and mashed)
½ tablespoon of light soy sauce
½ tablespoon of mirin
½ tablespoon of rice vinegar

First prepare the prawn tempura. Remove the heads and shells from the prawns. I like to leave the tails on because you can hold them when dropping the prawns into the oil for deep-frying. De-vein the backs of the prawns with a skewer or toothpick. Clean the prawns under cold running water and pat dry with paper towels or a tea towel. Season with salt and pepper. Pull and stretch the prawns out gently to straighten them.

Beat the water and egg together in a bowl, combining them thoroughly. Make sure that the mixture is very cold. Sift the plain flour, cornflour and baking powder into a bowl and mix together. Add the flour mixture to the water and egg little by little, folding it together with chopsticks and being careful not to over-mix. This will make a very light and crisp tempura batter. Heat the oil to 160–170°C in a deep frying pan or wok. Dip each prawn in the batter, then drop into the oil immediately and deep-fry for a few minutes until they are a golden-brown colour.

Bring a large saucepan of water to the boil, add the noodles, and cook for 4–5 minutes. Every time the pan begins to foam, add a cup of cold water to prevent the foam from overflowing. The cold water helps to

keep the noodles al dente. Drain them in a colander and rinse under cold running water. Drain again and toss with the vegetable oil to prevent the noodles from sticking. Pat them dry with a tea towel or paper towel.

To make the ume sauce, put all the ingredients into a small bowl and mix very well.

Place a whole nori sheet shiny side down at the bottom of the sushi mat, with the lines of the sheet lying horizontally across the mat. Look for the 2nd line from the top of the nori sheet, about 3–4 cm down. Keeping the top 3–4cm of the sheet clear, gradually place half the noodles in a very thin layer, horizontally, over the nori. Place 2 tablespoons of cress in the middle of the noodles, then put two pieces of prawn tempura in a single line on top.

To roll your sushi, follow the instructions on pages 112–13. Repeat with the remaining nori sheet and filling ingredients, and then cut each roll into 8–10 pieces (see page 113). Serve the ume sauce alongside, as a dipping sauce.

Tips
- Leftover ume sauce is delicious with steamed chicken or cooked prawn salad.
- It is important to keep all the batter ingredients cold. Make sure you keep the water, egg and flour in the fridge before mixing.

TSUKE-MAGURO, OKURA AND SHISO SOBA SUSHI
Marinated tuna with okra and shiso leaves soba sushi
浸けマグロとオクラ, しそ蕎麦寿司

Japanese summers are not only hot but also very humid, so many people don't want to eat heavy meals. I created this recipe during a scorching summer a few years ago, when it was so hot that I lost my appetite. It is the perfect light, cooling summer dish.

Japanese people eat many different types of noodles served cold, including udon, somen, hiyamugi, ramen and soba. They are fantastic with summer vegetables, especially my favourite summer vegetable, okra. Although okra is originally from South East Asia, Ethiopia and West Africa, it is a very popular vegetable in Japan for tempura or as a topping for tofu.

Makes 2 rolls (16–20 pieces)
a sushi mat (if using a bamboo mat, cover it tightly with cling film)
80–100g fresh, sashimi-quality tuna steak, 1cm thick (ask your fishmonger to prepare it for you)
1 teaspoon of sea salt
6–8 okra
120g dried soba noodles
1 teaspoon of vegetable oil
2 sheets of nori
4 shiso leaves

For the tuna marinade
½ tablespoon of wasabi paste
2 tablespoons of tamari soy sauce

1 tablespoon of mirin
1 tablespoon of sake

Slice the tuna steak lengthways into 1cm-wide strips. You should get two 20cm-long strips from an 80–100g slice of tuna steak (although you may need to use a larger number of shorter strips, depending on the shape of your steak). Put all the tuna marinade ingredients into a bowl and mix well. Add the sliced tuna and marinate for 5 to 24 hours in the fridge, covering the bowl with cling film.

Add the salt to a medium saucepan of water and bring to the boil. Add the okra and cook for 3 minutes until they are tender but firm. Be careful not to overcook them. Drain them in a colander and rinse under cold running water. Drain again, and cut the top and tail off each okra.

Bring a large saucepan of water to the boil, add the noodles, and cook for 4–5 minutes. Every time the pan begins to foam, add a cup of cold water to prevent the foam from overflowing. The cold water helps to keep the noodles al dente. Drain them in a colander and rinse under cold running water. Drain again and toss with vegetable oil to prevent the noodles from sticking. Pat them dry with a tea towel or paper towel.

Place a whole nori sheet shiny side down at the bottom of the sushi mat, with the lines of the sheet lying horizontally across the mat. Look for the 2nd line from the top of the nori sheet, about 3–4cm down. Keeping the top 3–4cm of the sheet clear, gradually place half the noodles in a very thin layer, horizontally, over the nori. Place 2 shiso leaves, one

20cm-long strip of tuna, and 3–4 pieces of okra side by side in the middle of the noodles, along the length of the nori. You can add some wasabi to the middle of the noodles before you add the other ingredients, if you like.

To roll your sushi, follow the instructions on pages 112–13. Repeat with the remaining nori sheet and filling ingredients, and then cut each roll into 8–10 pieces (see page 113).

Tips
- This tuna marinade works very well with wider strips of tuna, which you can eat with rice or salad.
- Okra is lovely with plain Japanese rice and a fresh tofu salad. Just cook the okra, chop it very thinly and mix with a dash of soy sauce.

INARI SUSHI

稲荷寿司

Inari is a popular sushi that uses braised abura-age, which is made from very thin slices of tofu – great for vegetarians. The abura-age is deep-fried first at 110°C, then deep-fried a second time at 180°C so that it becomes fluffy and looks like little pockets. In Japan, you would normally buy abura-age at supermarkets rather than make it yourself from fresh tofu. It is available chilled or frozen, and there are 3 pieces in each pack. You cut each piece crossways in half to make square pockets, giving you 6 inari skins per pack.

Inari skins have a sweet soy flavour, so you don't need nori, wasabi or soy sauce for dipping. I also use slightly less sushi-su (sushi vinegar) and less sugar and salt when making the sushi rice for inari sushi, as the inari skin already has a strong flavour. Once you have filled the inari skin with the sushi rice it will look like a pillow.

For the inari sushi rice (makes approximately 700g)

70ml rice vinegar or brown rice vinegar
1 tablespoon of sugar
1 teaspoon of sea salt
2 Japanese cups (300g) of Japanese rice
2 Japanese cups (360ml) of water

To make the sushi-su, put the rice vinegar, sugar and salt into a pan and leave on a low heat until the salt and sugar have dissolved. Be careful not to let it boil or the flavour will spoil. Remove from the heat and leave to cool.

To make the rice, first wash it thoroughly in a sieve for 4 minutes, gently turning it over by hand until the water runs clear. Drain the rice and put it into a pan with the water. Leave it to stand for a minimum of 30 minutes. It can be left overnight, but for best results I recommend leaving it for 30 minutes to 1 hour.

Leaving the water in the pan, bring the rice to the boil, put the lid on and reduce the heat, letting it simmer for 8–9 minutes. Turn the heat off and let it stand with the lid on for a further 15 minutes. Do not open the lid.

Put the rice into a wide flat dish such as a sushi oke, a baking dish or a roasting tray. Pour the sushi-su over the rice and fold it carefully into the rice with a wooden spoon as it cools down, being careful not to damage the grains. You can use a fan or a hairdryer on the coolest setting to speed up the cooling process, directing it at the rice. The sushi-su gives the rice more flavour and that familiar sticky glazed look.

If you don't want to use the rice immediately, cover it with cling film or a damp cloth so that it doesn't dry out. Leave in a cool place, but do not refrigerate. The fridge will make the rice texture hard and dry, and the sushi-su helps to preserve the rice without refrigeration. It will keep for a day.

For the inari skins (makes 12 inari)

6 abura-age
300ml kombu dashi (see recipe on page 156)
2 tablespoons of brown sugar
2 tablespoons of mirin
3 tablespoons of soy sauce

Blanch the abura-age for five seconds in boiling water (they float, so push them under or turn them over) and dry them with paper towels to remove some of the oil. Pour the dashi into a large saucepan and bring it to the boil, then add the brown sugar, mirin and soy sauce and reduce the heat. Add the abura-age to the pot and simmer for 10 minutes. Remove from the heat and let them cool in the liquid.

Take the braised abura-age (the inari skins) from the pot, squeeze out the stock and cut each one in half to make 12 square pockets in total. Open each pocket gently and fill with the sushi rice, so that it looks like a small pillow. These are plain inari, which are delicious, but you can also use different fillings – see the rest of this chapter for some great ideas.

Tips
- Inari skins break very easily, so be careful when you are filling them with rice or other ingredients.
- Inari sushi is perfect for picnics or lunch boxes.

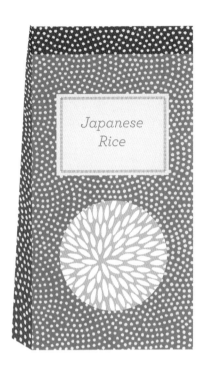

HIJIKI INARI SUSHI
Sea-vegetable inari sushi
ひじき稲荷寿司

Cooking the hijiki with kombu dashi (kelp stock) gives it a very gentle and clean flavour. Inari skins already have a sweet soy flavour, so the hijiki doesn't need to be cooked with lots of seasoning. I love the crunchy texture of the mangetout, which contrasts with the soft texture of the sea vegetables.

Makes 6 inari
25g dried hijiki
1 teaspoon of sea salt
6 mangetout
1 medium carrot

1 tablespoon of vegetable oil
100ml kombu dashi (see recipe on page 156)
1 tablespoon of soy sauce
1 tablespoon of mirin
1 tablespoon of sake
270g inari sushi rice (see recipe on page 122)
6 inari skins (see recipe on page 122)

Put the dried hijiki into cold water for about 15–20 minutes, then rinse and drain them well. Add the salt to a small saucepan of water and bring to the boil. Add the mangetout and cook for 1–2 minutes, until they are tender but still firm. Immediately drain them and plunge them into a bowl of cold water. Drain again and slice diagonally into thin julienne pieces. Peel the carrot and slice it lengthways into thin julienne strips, about 2mm x 15mm.

Heat the vegetable oil in a non-stick frying pan and sauté the hijiki and carrot for a few minutes. Add the kombu dashi, soy sauce, mirin and sake, and simmer until the liquid has reduced (around 10 minutes), being careful not to let it burn. Allow the braised hijiki to cool to room temperature, then mix with the rice and the mangetout. Fill the inari skins with the mixture, using approximately a sixth of the mixture per skin.

Tip
- The recipe on page 156 is for 800ml of kombu stock. You can keep the stock you don't use in the fridge for a couple of days, or freeze it in an ice-cube tray and use it in soups or sauces.

GOMA-AE INARI SUSHI

Spinach with white sesame inari sushi
胡麻和え稲荷寿司

Goma-ae – spinach with white sesame sauce – is a classic Japanese salad. It goes very well with inari skins, as the sesame seeds add a beautiful nutty taste. You can also serve it as a salad or a side dish.

Makes 6 inari
150–200g fresh spinach
1 teaspoon of sea salt
a dash of soy sauce
a dash of white sesame sauce (see recipe below)
6 inari skins (see recipe on page 122)
270g inari sushi rice (see recipe on page 122)

For the white sesame sauce
4 tablespoons of toasted white sesame seeds
1 teaspoon of brown sugar
½ tablespoon of mirin
½ tablespoon of soy sauce
1 tablespoon of water

Wash the spinach under cold running water. Add the salt to a large saucepan of water and bring to the boil. Put the spinach into the boiling water and cook for 1 minute (the cooking time will depend on the spinach leaves: some are very soft, but Japanese or Asian spinach is tougher). Make sure that it does not overcook. The leaves will turn dark green when they are ready.

Drain the spinach and rinse with cold water, then squeeze out the excess water and place the spinach on a paper towel. Drizzle with a little soy sauce, which will stop any more water coming out of the spinach – but don't put too much on!

To make the sauce, put the sesame seeds into a pestle and mortar, or a surikogi and suribachi, and grind them into a paste. Gradually add the sugar, mirin, soy sauce and water.

Chop the cooked spinach and toss it with the sauce in a bowl. Cover half of each of the inari skins with the inari sushi rice, then put the goma-ae on top.

Tips
- Leftover goma-ae is great as a side dish or for lunch boxes.
- You can use the sauce with asparagus, green beans or broccoli instead of spinach.

SASHIMI

さしみ

Sashimi is fresh raw fish and seafood, sliced into thin pieces and served with wasabi, soy and different types of sauces. It has to be very fresh and you must find a reliable place to buy it. If you find sushi- or sashimi-quality fish or seafood, see pages 145–51 for instructions on how to prepare it.

Sashimi always uses simple garnishes such as shiso leaves, shredded daikon (tsuma) or salad leaves. These are very important not only for their appearance but also because they clean the mouth and have a refreshing flavour.

SALMON SASHIMI
WITH PONZU SAUCE
サーモンさしみ　ポン酢

Ponzu sauce is very popular in Japan. You can buy it ready-made and most Japanese homes keep some in the fridge. If you make it yourself, you need to make it 24 hours before you want to use it. I love it with fresh warm tofu, as a dipping sauce for gyoza dumplings or to accompany a simple green salad and tomatoes. Here, the richness of the salmon is balanced by the citric sharpness of the ponzu. Finely shredded daikon (tsuma), or Japanese radish, is the perfect garnish.

Serves 4
ponzu sauce (see recipe below)
150–200g fresh, sashimi-quality salmon fillet, skinned and boned (ask your fishmonger to do this for you)
10cm-long piece of daikon (Japanese radish), or mooli
a handful of cress, to garnish

For the ponzu sauce (makes approximately 175ml)
100ml tamari soy sauce
100ml lime juice
2 tablespoons of mirin
3cm x 3cm piece of dried kombu (kelp)
a handful of katsuobushi (bonito flakes)

Remember to make the ponzu sauce a day before you need it. Mix all the ingredients together in a small bowl and keep in the fridge for 24 hours to rest. Strain the sauce through a fine sieve into a container or bottle.

You can keep the ponzu sauce in the fridge for a few weeks. When it gets cloudy and loses its shine, it's time to throw it out.

Place the salmon fillet on a chopping board. Holding your knife at a 20-degree angle, start to slice the fish from one end into 0.5cm-thick bite-size pieces, supporting the salmon lightly with the fingers of your other hand. Make sure you cut each slice in one smooth action – do not use a sawing motion or too much force (see bottom photo on page 146).

If you are confident with your knife skills, you can slice your daikon using the 'Katsura slice'. Hold the daikon and peel it very carefully in a circular direction using a sharp knife – as though you are peeling the skin off an apple. Keep turning the knife around the daikon, slicing until it is all finished, or just do as much as you can. The slices should be very thin – 2mm thick – and look like a sheet of paper. You could also use a potato peeler to do this. If you are using a Japanese mandolin or slicer, peel the daikon, then slice or shred it very thinly.

Slice your sheet-like pieces of daikon as thinly as you can, so that it is like string. Then soak it in cold water for 10 minutes and drain very well.

Mix a handful of the shredded daikon with the cress and place in the centre of the plate, then arrange the sashimi pieces around it. Serve the ponzu on the side, and drizzle it over the fish before eating.

Tips
• Ponzu sauce can be useful for many things and keeps well, so make a generous amount.

- Use a very sharp knife to cut the fish – I recommend using a Japanese sashimi knife.
- Try different types of fish or shellfish.

TUNA TATAKI AND YAKUMI
Seared tuna with Japanese herb sauce
マグロのたたきと薬味

Tuna sashimi is the most common sashimi dish, but seared tuna tataki is also wonderful. It is very important to have a good sauce for tataki. Yakumi has a variety of Oriental herbs in it: shiso, the Japanese chive 'wakegi', and ginger. Japanese people believe that herbs are good for your health: *yaku* means 'medicine' and *mi*, 'taste'.

Serves 4
2 x 200g fresh, sushi-quality tuna steaks, 2cm thick (ask your fishmonger to prepare them for you)
1 tablespoon of vegetable oil
a handful of cress, to garnish
10cm-long piece of celery, very thinly sliced, to garnish

For the yakumi (makes approximately 200g)
1 large clove of garlic, peeled
2cm-long piece of ginger, peeled and roughly chopped
1 shallot, peeled and roughly chopped
10 shiso leaves
3 spring onions
15ml rice vinegar
30ml light soy sauce
60ml rapeseed or olive oil
½ teaspoon of sugar
a pinch of sea salt

To make the sauce, crush the garlic, ginger and shallot in a pestle and mortar, or a surikogi and suribachi. Roughly chop the shiso leaves and spring onions, and add them to the mortar, then pour in the rice vinegar, lime juice, soy sauce, oil, sugar and salt, until it becomes a sauce. You could also use a food processor or hand blender, which is much quicker.

Place the tuna steaks on a plate and pat dry with a paper towel. Heat the vegetable oil in a non-stick frying pan, and sear both sides of the tuna in the pan until the steaks change colour to white, about 5–7 seconds on each side. Place the tuna in cold water, quickly rinse it and then pat dry with paper towels.

To slice the tuna for sashimi, place the fish on a chopping board and look for the grain of the muscle. You need to cut across the grain, not with it. Holding your knife at a 20-degree angle, start to slice the tuna from one end into 1.5cm-thick bite-size pieces, supporting the steak lightly with the fingers of your other hand. Make sure you cut each slice in one smooth action – do not use a sawing motion or too much force.

Pour half the sauce on a plate, then arrange the slices of tuna on top, and garnish with the cress and thinly sliced celery. Serve the remaining sauce on the side.

Tips
- The sauce can be made a few hours ahead and kept in the fridge, so that the flavour develops.

- If you use coriander instead of shiso you will need a good handful to give the sauce its green colour.
- Beef steak also works well with the sauce.

TAI SASHIMI WITH MIKAN CHILLI SAUCE AND MIZUNA

Sea-bream sashimi with satsuma chilli sauce and mizuna leaves
鯛さしみスパイシーみかんソース

Satsuma, also called a satsuma mandarin, is a very popular citrus fruit in England. We call it mikan in Japanese (Satsuma is the name of the province in South Japan where they are grown). Satsumas arrived in Western countries hundreds of years ago from the Japanese embassies. I remember the first time I saw satsumas in an English supermarket, I could not believe my eyes and had to buy some immediately to remind me of home.

Serves 4
satsuma chilli sauce (see recipe below)
2 fillets (140–150g each) of fresh, sashimi-
  quality sea bream, skinned and boned (ask
  your fishmonger to do this, or see page 149)
a handful of mizuna, to garnish

For the satsuma chilli sauce
1 satsuma or ¼ of an orange
2 teaspoons of sweet chilli sauce
juice of ½ a lime
juice of ½ a lemon
1½ tablespoons of light soy sauce

½ a clove of garlic, grated
1cm-long piece of ginger, grated
1 tablespoon of peanut or olive oil

To make the sauce, cut the satsuma in half and squeeze the juice into a small bowl or jar, then add the other ingredients and mix well. Leave for 15 minutes, then strain the liquid into a bowl.

Rinse the sea-bream fillet under cold running water and place on a chopping board. Holding the knife at a 20-degree angle, start to slice the fish from one end into 0.5cm-thick bite-size pieces, supporting the fish lightly with the index finger of your other hand. Make sure you cut each slice in one smooth action – do not use a sawing motion or too much force.

Once you have sliced both fillets, place the sashimi slices in a small bowl of cold water with ice cubes for a few minutes. The sashimi will become slightly white in colour. This makes it taste fresh and gives it a good texture. Drain the fish and pat it dry with paper towels.

Put the mizuna in the centre of a plate, and place the sea-bream sashimi around the mizuna. Serve the sauce on the side, and drizzle it over the fish before eating.

Tips
- You can try different raw fish or shellfish: salmon, tuna, sea bass and scallop all work well, as does cooked prawn.
- You can use rocket, baby spinach or cress instead of mizuna.

KORYORI & SOUP

Small Dishes & Soup
小料理と汁物

When you go to a sushi restaurant, some interesting small dishes, called koryori, arrive at the beginning of the meal – like Japanese tapas. I love to have some nibbles with a drink while thinking about which sushi to order or chatting with the chef in front of the sushi bar. The small dishes may be pickles, slow-cooked vegetables, a seafood and vegetable salad. They must be small with a light flavour, because the main reason for going to a sushi restaurant or making sushi at home is to eat the sushi!

KURO GOMA-AE

Green beans with black sesame sauce
胡麻和え

Goma-ae is a very popular Japanese home-cooked dish. I love the aroma of the black sesame seeds and the sweet and nutty flavour of the sauce. Use a surikogi and suribachi or a regular pestle and mortar to grind the sesame seeds. I always cut the beans in half, because it is better to have bite-size pieces of food when eating with chopsticks.

Serves 4
200g green beans
1 tablespoon of sea salt

For the black sesame sauce
4 tablespoons of black sesame seeds
1 tablespoon of mirin
½ tablespoon of soy sauce
1 teaspoon of miso
1 tablespoon of brown sugar
1 tablespoon of water

Trim the ends off the green beans, cut the beans in half and wash them in cold water. Add the salt to a saucepan of water and bring to the boil. Cook the beans for 2 minutes or until tender. Do not overcook – it's important to keep them crunchy! Drain the beans in a colander and rinse with cold running water to cool them down. Drain again and leave them to dry.

To make the sauce, crush the sesame seeds in a surikogi and suribachi or pestle and mortar, grinding them into a paste.

Gradually add the mirin, soy sauce and miso, mixing continuously. Add the sugar and water. Toss the green beans with the sauce and serve.

Tips
- Asparagus, spinach, broccoli or cauliflower all work well instead of green beans.
- The sauce keeps well in the fridge for 3 days.

CUCUMBER, WAKAME AND PRAWN SALAD WITH JAPANESE MUSTARD AND SESAME SAUCE
キュウリ、わかめ茹でエビのからし胡麻ソース

English and Japanese mustard are very similar, so when I make this sauce I often use the English mustard which I keep in my fridge. I have not made this recipe too spicy, so you can add more mustard if you would like it to be hotter. This dish uses mixed sea vegetables, which are very tasty. Packets of dried sea-vegetable mix are available in many Japanese and Asian supermarkets, as well as in health-food stores or online.

Serves 4
¾–1 cucumber
a pinch of sea salt
a small handful of dried sea-vegetable mix, or dried wakame
2 shiso leaves
8–12 cooked prawns, peeled, tails on
optional: a handful of cress, to garnish

For the Japanese mustard and sesame sauce
1½ tablespoons of sesame paste (tahini)
1 teaspoon of brown sugar
1 tablespoon of soy sauce
2 tablespoons of rice vinegar or brown rice vinegar
¼ teaspoon of Japanese or English mustard
1 tablespoon of water

Slice the ends off a cucumber and cut it lengthways into quarters. Remove the seeds carefully with a spoon or knife. Cut the cucumber quarters very thinly into 2mm diagonal slices and leave them in a bowl with a pinch of salt for 10 minutes. Soak the sea-vegetable mix or dried wakame in another bowl of water for 15 minutes or until it opens out and becomes soft.

Put the cucumber and sea-vegetable mix or wakame in a colander, drain them and squeeze out the excess water. Slice the shiso leaves very finely. Put the cucumber, sea vegetables and shiso into a bowl and mix together.

Put the ingredients for the sauce into a bowl and mix well until creamy.

To serve, put the cucumber salad on a plate or dish, place the cooked prawns on top and then drizzle over the sauce. Garnish with cress, if you like.

Tips
- I love to use cooked squid or tofu instead of the prawns.
- When you soften sea vegetables in water, they will expand up to 5 times or more in size, so be careful not to use too much or you will end up with a huge amount!
- The sauce will keep in the fridge for 3 days. If it gets too thick you can add a small amount of water to thin it.

SUNOMONO
Cucumber and squid salad with
sanbai-su dressing
酢の物

Sunomono is a simple cucumber salad, which you may have seen on the menu in Japanese restaurants. The dressing, sanbai-su, contains the three core ingredients of rice vinegar, soy sauce and sugar. I like to add dashi and mirin, for a more gentle, subtle and sophisticated flavour.

Serves 4
1 x 150g squid, cleaned (ask your fishmonger
to do this for you)
¾–1 cucumber
a pinch of sea salt
2–3 shiso leaves, sliced, to garnish
white sesame seeds, to garnish

For the sanbai-su dressing
2 tablespoons of rice vinegar or brown rice
vinegar
60ml katsuo dashi (see recipe on page 156)
2 teaspoons of light soy sauce
½ teaspoon of brown sugar
1 tablespoon of mirin

To make the sanbai-su sauce, put all the ingredients into a small bowl and mix together. Put to one side to cool down.

To prepare the squid, remove the tentacles and rinse them under cold running water. Slice the body into 1cm-wide rings. Bring a large saucepan of water to the boil. Add the sliced squid and tentacles and cook for 2–3 minutes, until it turns milky white. Drain and pat dry with a tea towel or paper towels. Put the cooked squid into the sauce to marinate while preparing the rest of the dish.

Slice the ends off the cucumber and cut it in half lengthways. Remove the seeds carefully with a spoon or a knife, then slice the cucumber very thinly into half-moon shapes. Place in a bowl, sprinkle with salt and mix thoroughly. Leave for 5–10 minutes, then squeeze the cucumber very well with both hands.

Place the cucumber into a small dish or bowl, then pour the sauce and marinated squid on top. Garnish with the sliced shiso leaves and sesame seeds.

Tip
- Use cooked octopus, prawns or crabmeat instead of squid.

CLAM MISO SOUP
アサリのみそ汁

Some traditional Japanese people have miso soup with every meal, and a lot of restaurants serve it for free as part of the menu. You can use a variety of ingredients for miso soup – mix it with vegetables, mushrooms or shellfish, and choose your favourite dashi, or stock. It is important to use good-quality stock and miso.

To serve 4 as a side dish (makes
    approximately 900g)
300–350g clams
600ml cold water
5cm-long piece of dried kombu (kelp)
3 tablespoons of white miso paste
4 teaspoons of chopped chives, to garnish

Ask your fishmonger if the clams have been cleaned. If not, place them in a bowl with plenty of salted water – 1 tablespoon of salt to 500ml of water. Leave them in the fridge or a cool dark place for at least 1 hour, so that they release any sand. Rub the shells with your fingers to clean them. Throw away any that are slightly open, as these may be bad, then rinse the rest under cold running water and drain well.

Pour 600ml of cold water into a large saucepan. Put a piece of dried kombu into the pan and leave for 30 minutes until the kombu expands and softens. Add the clams to the pan and start heating up on a medium heat. When it begins to boil, turn down the heat and remove and discard the kombu. Skim off any scum from the surface. By this time, the clams should be open – discard any that aren't.

Scoop out some of the stock from the pan using a ladle and put into a small bowl. Add the miso paste to the bowl and stir until it dissolves. Gradually add the diluted miso to the soup, stirring gently. Remove from the heat.

Serve in small soup bowls and garnish with chopped chives.

Tips
- Use different types of clams or shellfish.
- There are lots of varieties of miso available, such as hatcho miso and brown rice miso – see Glossary, pages 17–18 – so experiment and see which one you like best.
- Do not overcook the soup as this will ruin the flavour.

Preparing Fish & Seafood

As mentioned in the introduction, it is very important to buy sushi- or sashimi-quality fish and seafood to make sushi and sashimi. Therefore, you need to find a fishmonger you can trust. This doesn't necessarily have to be a Japanese fishmonger. A good fishmonger on the high street will do just as well.

SALMON

Salmon is a very popular oily fish, and a rich source of fatty acids such as omega-3 and omega-6, as well as being high in protein and vitamins. I enjoy eating all types of salmon: raw as sushi and sashimi; marinated then grilled or roasted; poached or steamed; and, of course, smoked. Salmon comes from a variety of sources – wild, Pacific and Atlantic, farm-raised and organic – but whichever you choose, always try to buy sustainable salmon. There are a few other things to look for when you buy salmon:

- The skin should be clean and shiny, not slimy.
- The gills should be bright pink or bright red.
- The eyes should be clear, not muddy.
- The fish should smell of the sea or salt, but not smell fishy.

Preparing salmon

When buying salmon from a fishmonger to make sushi or sashimi, you can ask them to fillet and skin the fish for you. This will be much easier for you, and you can just order the size that you need. If you want to make a large amount of sushi though, you can buy a whole fish and cut slices from it yourself.

We call the method of cutting a fish into three parts – two fillets and the backbone sanmai-oroshi in Japanese. You will need a very sharp boning knife to do this. Place the fish on a chopping board, hold the fish head with one hand, put the knife behind the gills and cut down vertically until the knife reaches the backbone. Turn the fish over and do the same on the other side, but this time cut through the bone to remove the head completely. Slice the belly open with the knife, take out the guts and clean the fish under cold running water, then pat it dry with a paper towel or tea towel.

You can then remove the first fillet: place the fish on the chopping board so that its belly is facing you, hold the knife and start slicing from the tail to the head, with the knife just touching the backbone. To remove the other fillet, do not turn the fish over, but put the knife under the backbone at the tail end and, keeping the knife very close to the bone, start slicing along its length. You can then remove the bone completely. Rinse the fillets well under cold running water.

Next, skin the salmon. Place the salmon fillet on a chopping board skin side down with the tail end closest to you. Make a small cut at the tail end, stopping just before you reach the skin. Then, holding the knife at a 20-degree angle, and the flap of skin with your other hand, slide the knife all the way along, above the skin. You should hold the fish very tightly when sliding the knife.

Slicing salmon

When buying salmon for sushi rolls, ask your fishmonger to cut it into a 1cm-thick fillet, which you can then slice into long, 1cm-wide strips. One 180–200g piece of salmon fillet is enough for 4 sushi rolls.

To slice salmon for sashimi, place the fillet on a chopping board. Holding your knife at a 20-degree angle, start slicing the salmon from one end into 0.5cm-thick, bite-size pieces, supporting the salmon lightly with the fingers of your other hand. Make sure you cut each slice in one smooth action – do not use a sawing motion or too much force. (See bottom photo on page 146.)

Tip

- The bones can be used for making stock and any leftover pieces from making sushi can be grilled.

TUNA

Tuna (*maguro* in Japanese) is a huge saltwater fish with a very meaty flavour. Most people wouldn't buy a whole tuna as they are much too big, and instead buy a piece of loin or a slice like a steak. There are lots of different types of tuna; bluefin tuna is the most common type and popular for sushi and sashimi in Japanese restaurants (about 80 per cent of tuna used in this way is bluefin), although yellowfin tuna is also popular.

A whole tuna will be bought by a Japanese fishmonger or a sushi restaurant, where it will be cut into two parts. Akami (pronounced *ah-kah-me*) is the very lean, bright red meat from the sides of the tuna and is the most common part. Toro (*to-roh*) is the fatty part of the tuna, taken from the belly, and is considered to be the best part of the fish. Toro is further broken up into two subtypes, chutoro and ohtoro. *Chu* means 'medium', and chutoro is a mixture of lean and fatty parts, with a good balance of richness. Ohtoro is the fattiest part of tuna (*oh* means 'extremely'); it has a very rich buttery flavour and melts in the mouth but is very expensive, so is best kept for a special treat.

Unfortunately tuna is not a sustainable fish, especially bluefin. When you buy or order tuna at the fishmonger or a restaurant, you may be offered albacore or yellowfin tuna, which can sometimes be from more sustainable stocks, depending on the source. Although albacore tuna is not traditionally used for sushi or sashimi as it has white meat, it is as rich in flavour as bluefin or yellowfin tuna.

One great thing about sushi is that you need only a very small portion of tuna for each serving. One 180–200g piece of tuna steak is enough for 4 sushi rolls.

Slicing tuna

When buying tuna for sushi rolls, ask your fishmonger to cut it into a 1cm-thick steak, which you can then slice into long, 1cm-wide strips.

To slice tuna for sashimi, place the tuna steak on a chopping board and look for the grain of the muscle. You need to cut across the grain, not with it. Holding your knife at a 20-degree angle, start slicing the fish from one end into 0.5cm-thick, bite-size pieces, supporting the steak lightly with the fingers of your other hand. Make sure you cut each slice in one smooth action – do not use a sawing motion or too much force. (See photos on page 148.)

• I recommend buying sustainable tuna, so ask your fishmonger whether the fish is from sustainable stocks.

SMALL AND MEDIUM FISH (HERRING, MACKEREL, RED SNAPPER, SARDINES, SEA BASS, SEA BREAM)

HERRING
Herring is a very popular and sustainable fish, great smoked or with a strongly flavoured sauce.

MACKEREL
Mackerel is a common and popular fish in both the UK and Japan. It has a strong flavour and is a wonderful source of nutrition, containing omega-3 fatty acids, vitamin B12 and selenium. It goes well with radish, lemon or vinegar as these sharp, acidic flavours cut through the rich oiliness of the fish.

RED SNAPPER
Similar to sea bream, red snapper is a light and mild fish and very common in Japan.

SARDINES
Similar to mackerel but smaller, sardines have a rich, strong flavour. Great to serve with ginger or herbs.

SEA BASS
Slightly more pricey than sea bream, sea bass has a rich taste and great flavour and is suitable for any kind of cooking method.

SEA BREAM

Sea bream is very popular and reasonably priced in the UK. It has a very light taste and goes with any sauce.

Preparing the fish

To fillet small or medium fish sanmai-oroshi style, you will need a very sharp boning knife. Place the whole fish on a chopping board, hold the fish head with one hand, put the knife behind the gills and cut down vertically until the knife reaches the backbone. Turn the fish over and do the same on the other side, but this time cut through the bone to remove the head completely. Slice the belly open with the knife, take out the guts and clean the fish under cold running water, then pat it dry with a paper towel or tea towel.

Put the knife under the backbone at the head end and, keeping the knife very close to the bone, start slicing along its length towards the tail. Turn the fish over and do the same on the other side. You can then remove the backbone. Clean the fillets under cold running water and pat them dry.

Next, skin the fish. Place a fillet skin side down with the tail end closest to you. Make a small cut at the tail end, stopping just before you reach the skin. Then, holding the knife at a 20-degree angle, and the flap of skin with your other hand, slide the knife all the way along, above the skin. Run your fingers over the fish and you will be able to feel the pin bones in the flesh: use tweezers to pull these out.

Slicing the fish

To slice the fish for sashimi, place the skin side of the fillet on a clean chopping board. Hold the fillet firmly with your index and middle fingers. Place the knife at a diagonal angle across the fillet, facing away from your other hand, and start to slice the fillet very thinly.

Once you have sliced the entire fillet, put the sashimi slices into a small bowl of cold water with ice cubes and leave for a few minutes. The sashimi will become slightly white in colour. This makes it taste fresh and gives it a good texture. Drain the sashimi and pat dry with paper towels.

PRAWNS

Prawns are a high source of protein, are very low in fat and calories, and contain lots of omega-2, vitamin B12 and zinc, so can form part of a light, healthy diet. You will find many different types and sizes of prawns: from the very small, to large ones such as tiger or king prawns. Large prawns are useful for sushi, tempura and ebi furai.

I recommend buying fresh, raw prawns from the fishmonger – sometimes you can buy them when they are still alive. Many places sell frozen raw prawns, which are fine for stir-fries. Make sure you avoid any which have been cooked, shelled and then frozen, as they do not have as much flavour. When buying prawns:

- The shells should be firm and glossy, not broken or slippery.
- There should be no discolouration of the head and shell.
- They should smell fresh and salty like the sea; avoid if they smell at all unpleasant.

- The eyes should be present and shiny.
- Uncooked prawns are shiny grey, not pink.
- If they are pink, they have already been cooked.

Preparation for deep-frying:
tempura or ebi furai

Remove the heads and shells from the prawns. I like to leave the tails on the prawns because you can hold them when dropping the prawns into the oil for deep-frying. De-vein the backs of the prawns with a skewer or toothpick. Clean the prawns under cold running water and pat dry with paper towels or a tea towel. Pull and stretch the prawns out gently to straighten them.

Preparation for sushi

Do not remove the heads and shells. Hold a prawn with one hand and, pointing a skewer away from the head of the prawn, push the skewer between the shell and body towards the tail, making sure the prawn is straight. Repeat with the remaining prawns. Put plenty of water in a large saucepan, add salt and bring to the boil, then add the prawns and cook for about 2–3 minutes. They will turn bright pink when they are done. Do not overcook them or they will be tough. Remove the prawns from the saucepan and quickly rinse them under cold running water. Drain and place on paper towels and let them cool down completely.

Once cool, remove the skewers and carefully peel off the shells. I like to serve them with the heads and tails still on, but you might prefer to remove the heads. To butterfly the prawns, cut open the belly side with a knife, being careful not to cut right through, and open the prawns up so that they are lying flat.

CRAB

It is a great pleasure to buy a whole fresh crab. One of my favourite dishes is fresh crab from the north coast of Cornwall, served simply with cucumber salad. I understand that many people are not comfortable or confident handling a live crab, but don't worry – it isn't as difficult as you think.

I recommend killing the crab before cooking it because it causes less suffering and the meat will be more tender and less watery. After cooking, you can keep the crab in the fridge for a few days and use it in a variety of dishes. When buying a live crab from your fishmonger:
- Choose one which is lively and moving.
- Check that it hasn't been kept in a tank for longer than a week.
- Make sure that it smells of the sea, and that it doesn't smell fishy.

Preparing a live crab

Turn the crab on to its back. Look for the pointed flap towards the back of the shell. Lift this flap and you will see a tiny hole. Use a chopstick or metal skewer to stab into the hole towards the back of the shell.

Bring a large saucepan half full of water with a small handful of salt in it to the boil, and add the crab. When the water comes back to the boil, cook it for 10–15 minutes, depending on the size of the crab. Remove the pan from the heat and drain the boiling water carefully. Take out the cooked crab, and rinse and clean it under cold running water.

For sushi I use only the white meat, which is located in the claws and legs. Twist and pull off the claws and legs. Crack the shell with the base of a strong knife or a rolling pin and remove the white meat.

Place the crab body (the centre part) on the chopping board with the shell side down. Using your thumbs, push hard from the bottom of the core and lift the body section out. Trim the edges of the crab shell, and remove and discard the stomach sac, ten 'dead men's fingers', eyes and mouth part from inside.

Scrape off the brown meat. You can use this for salads or sandwiches, or, if you prefer, mix it with white meat and use it in sushi.

SCALLOPS

Scallops have an amazingly sweet flavour which adapts well to different cooking methods. I prefer to cook them as simply as possible, either by grilling or frying them, although my favourite method is to serve them raw, or briefly seared in a very hot pan.

They have beautiful shells, with rings on them. A new ring forms each year, the same as with a tree, and these tell you the age of the scallop. Most scallops for sale have already been removed from their shells, but try to buy them in their shell if you can as it's likely these will be much fresher. I recommend buying day-boat (caught within a day of harvest) or hand-dived (collected by hand) scallops, which are much higher quality and more environmentally friendly. When buying scallops:

- They should be clean with no smell and still moist.
- Only buy them in season: January to mid June in the UK.
- If you are keeping your scallops in the fridge, store them shell side down as this is the way they naturally sit.

Preparing scallops

To remove the scallop from the shell, hold the shell with a tea towel. Gently insert a scallop or shell knife at the front of the scallop and twist the knife to open and remove the top of the shell. Using a spoon, scrape the bottom of the scallop meat from the shell. Hold the meat in one hand and gently tear off the membrane with the other hand. Rinse the scallop under cold running water and drain well.

If you buy scallops without shells, you just need to wash them under cold running water, drain and gently pat them dry with paper towels. Remove the orange part, known as the 'coral'. Slice the scallops very thinly. It depends on their size, but you can usually get 4 thin slices from a medium-sized scallop.

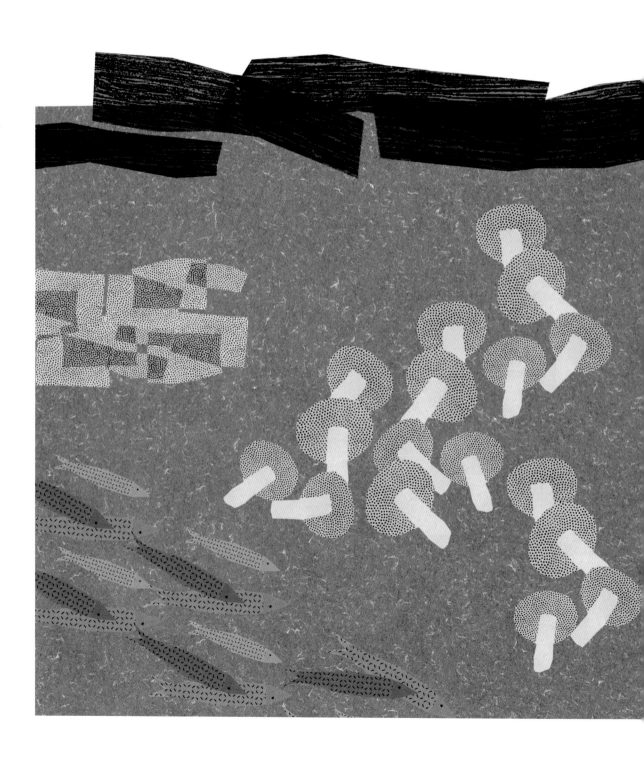

DASHI

Japanese Stock
出汁

Stock is used in most Japanese dishes, and most are made from dried ingredients including mushrooms, sea vegetables and fish – very different from Western stocks.

It is always better to use a home-made stock rather than an instant one, but the good news is that Japanese stocks are very quick to make compared to Western stocks – no more watching the pan simmer for 4 hours. The flavours are generally extracted by infusion, and each stock has its own unique taste and aroma. In this chapter I have included a selection of Japanese stocks – I hope you will find your favourite!

AWASE DASHI
Dried kelp and bonito-flake stock
合わせ出汁 一番出汁と二番出汁

Awase means 'combination', and this stock is a combination of dried kombu (kelp) and katsuobushi (bonito fish flakes). There are two types of awase dashi, depending on the quality: ichiban dashi and niban dashi. Ichiban dashi is a very high-quality stock, identified by its wonderful aroma and delicate flavour. Brewed quickly, it is a beautiful clear stock, like a French consommé soup, and is normally used for Japanese clear soup (suimono) or light, delicate sauces.

Niban dashi is made by reusing the kombu and katsuobushi from ichiban dashi. As ichiban dashi is made very quickly, there is still a lot of flavour left in the ingredients, and these can be infused again. Niban dashi is used for most common home-cooking dishes and is ideal for miso soup and teriyaki sauce.

For the ichiban dashi (makes approximately 800ml)
15cm x 15cm piece of dried kombu (kelp)
1 litre of cold water
3 handfuls (roughly 25g) of katsuobushi (bonito flakes)

Wipe the dried kombu with a clean cloth. Put the water into a large saucepan and add the kombu. Soak and infuse in the water for 30 minutes. You can tell when the kombu is hydrated as it will roughly double in size.

Put the pan over a medium heat and bring to the boil. As soon as it starts boiling, remove the kombu from the pan, put it to one side for the niban dashi and turn off the heat. You cannot keep boiling the kombu because it will become slimy and unclear.

Add the katsuobushi to the pan and leave until the flakes have sunk to the bottom of the pan completely, which should take about 10 minutes. Line a colander with paper towel, cheese cloth or muslin and strain the katsuobushi into a bowl, saving the flakes for niban dashi.

For the niban dashi (makes approximately 500ml)
leftover kombu (kelp) and katsuobushi (bonito flakes) from the ichiban dashi
600ml cold water
1 handful (roughly 8–10g) of katsuobushi

Put the leftover kombu and katsuobushi into a saucepan and add the water. Bring to the boil over a medium heat. When it starts boiling, remove from the heat and add one handful of katsuobushi to the pan. Leave until the flakes have sunk completely to the bottom of the pan. Line a colander with paper towel, cheese cloth or muslin and strain the liquid into a bowl. Discard the kombu and katsuobushi.

Tips
- When you strain the stock, do not squeeze the paper towel, cheese cloth or muslin, as this will make the stock cloudy and the flavour will be too strong.
- Keeps in the fridge for 2–3 days and the freezer for a week.

NIBOSHI DASHI
Dried baby-sardine stock
煮干し出汁

Niboshi dashi is made from dried baby sardines. It is a very common stock in Japan and is often used in family dishes. My grandmother would prepare the niboshi in a pan before going to bed every time I visited her house, so that she was ready to make miso soup for our breakfast. Niboshi dashi has a deep, strong flavour and goes really well with miso. It makes an absolutely amazing miso soup.

Makes 800ml
20g niboshi (dried sardines)
850ml cold water

Remove the heads and guts of the niboshi by pinching the head between your fingers and pulling it off – the guts should come out too. Put the niboshi and water into a large saucepan over a medium heat and bring it to the boil. When it starts to boil, turn down the heat and simmer for 5 minutes, skimming the foam off the top.

Remove from the heat. Line a colander with paper towel, cheese cloth or muslin and strain the liquid into a bowl. Discard the niboshi.

Tips
- When you strain the stock, do not squeeze the paper towel, cheese cloth or muslin, as this will make the stock cloudy and the flavour will be too strong.
- Keeps in the fridge for 2 days and the freezer for a week.
- When you buy niboshi, choose ones with a nice silver colour and a straight shape.

KATSUO DASHI
Bonito-flake stock
かつお出汁

Katsuo dashi is a very traditional Japanese stock that is unique in flavour and appearance. To make the katsuobushi (bonito flakes), the lean part of a block of bonito fillet is boiled and then smoked around 15 times, each time for 5–6 hours, and then shredded into flakes. It is absolutely full of umami! I normally make 800ml and use it in miso soups, noodle soups and teriyaki sauce.

Makes approximately 800ml
3 handfuls (roughly 25g) of katsuobushi
*   (bonito flakes)*
900ml–1 litre of cold water

Put the water into a large saucepan over a medium heat and bring to the boil. As soon as it starts boiling, turn off the heat. Add the katsuobushi to the pan, then leave until all the flakes have sunk to the bottom of the pan, which should take about 10 minutes.

   Line a colander with paper towel, cheese cloth or muslin and strain the liquid into a bowl. Discard the katsuobushi.

KOMBU DASHI
Dried kelp stock
昆布出汁

Kombu dashi is a clear, lightly flavoured stock made from dried kelp, a sea vegetable. It has a subtle and gentle flavour, reminiscent of the sea. It is not as strong as fish stocks such as niboshi (page 155) or katsuo (left), and is great for vegetarians. I use kombu dashi for Japanese noodle soups, and some rice dishes or hotpot dishes.

   You can buy kombu at some Western supermarkets and also from seaweed foragers in Scotland or Cornwall. It has a rich mineral and high nutrition level. You can eat the kombu after using it for the stock: the perfect snack for the hungry chef.

Makes 800ml
10cm x 15cm piece of kombu (dried kelp)
800ml cold water

Wipe the dried kombu with a clean cloth. Put the water into a large saucepan and soak the kombu for anything from 1 hour to overnight. It might affect the depth of flavour slightly if you soak it for longer than an hour, but most of the flavour comes out when you start boiling the water. Heat the water slowly and, just before it comes to the boil, remove the kombu and take the saucepan off the heat. The stock should look clear and have a beautiful sea aroma.

Tip
- You can keep the stock in the fridge for 2 days and the freezer for a week. When it gets old or goes off, it will look cloudy.

SHIITAKE-MUSHROOM DASHI
Dried shiitake-mushroom stock
干し椎茸出汁

Makes approximately 750ml stock
4–5 large dried shiitake mushrooms
4¼ Japanese cups (765ml) of cold water

Shiitake-mushroom dashi is my favourite stock and very easy to make. You can use the shiitake mushrooms afterwards for any of the recipes that require them. Sometimes I buy fresh shiitake mushrooms from my local supermarket and leave them in a dry place. It takes 5 days to a week for them to dry out completely. Once dry, you can keep them in an air-tight container for a long time. I love to make my own dried shiitake mushrooms, but you can also buy them ready-made from Asian supermarkets and some local supermarkets.

I use this stock not only for Japanese dishes, but also for pasta and risotto.

Put the cold water and dried shiitake mushrooms into a deep saucepan and soak the mushrooms for anything between 2 hours and overnight. If you are short of time, you can add hot water and soak the mushrooms for 10 minutes. Remove the mushrooms from the stock and squeeze them to remove any excess stock. Keep the mushrooms, as you can use them in other recipes – I love to make shiitake miso soup with tofu or wakame (sea vegetable).

Tips
- You can keep the stock in the fridge for 2 days and the freezer for a week.
- I recommend using cold water, as it makes a better-quality stock.
- For a stronger flavour and aroma, soak the mushrooms overnight.

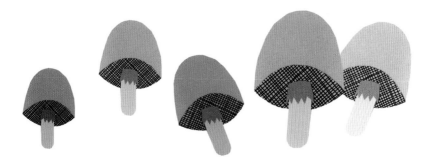

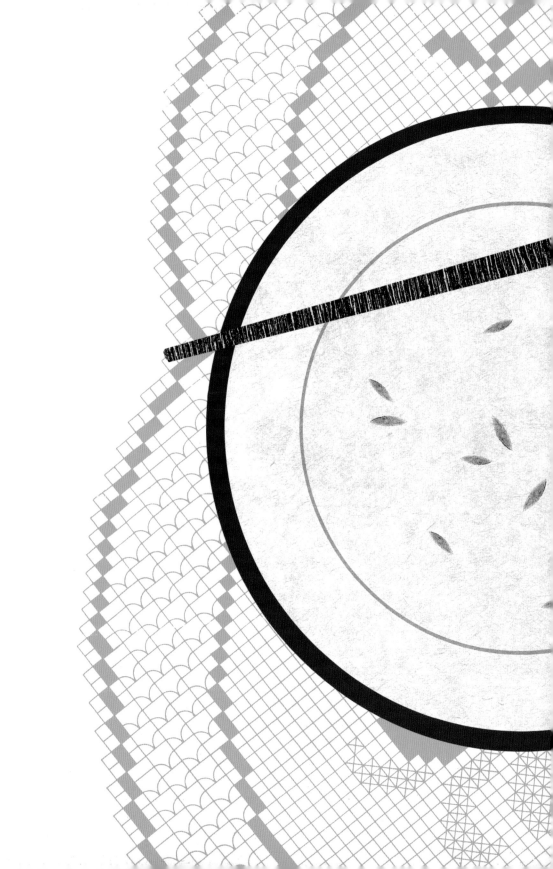

Stockists

Most supermarkets now stock everything you need to make your own sushi, but here are some useful websites for ethical and sushi-grade fish, and for Japanese products.

Fish
www.ethicalshellfishcompany.co.uk
www.kazari.co.uk
www.martins-seafresh.co.uk
www.moxonsfreshfish.com

Japanese food products
www.atariya.co.uk
www.clearspring.co.uk
www.mitoku.com

Japanese food products, tableware and kitchenware
www.cookingjapanese.co.uk
www.muji.eu (sushi omelette pan)
www.japancentre.com
www.japanesekitchen.co.uk
www.sushisushi.co.uk

Menu Plans

You can easily combine the recipes in this book to make a variety of meals (sometimes it might be most cost-effective to make a couple of recipes that include the same type of fish), but here are a few ideas for menus for all occasions.

Canapés for a party of around 35

Kappa maki
Cucumber small roll
(4 rolls / 24–32 pieces)

Tekka maki
Tuna and wasabi small roll
(4 rolls / 24–32 pieces)

Daikon oshinko maki
Pickled Japanese radish small roll
(4 rolls / 24–32 pieces)

Simple avocado ura hosomaki
Avocado with black sesame seeds small inside-out roll
(4 rolls / 24 pieces)

Classic vegetable futomaki
Dashi-maki tamago, braised shiitake mushrooms, carrots and cucumber giant roll
(2 rolls / 16–20 pieces)

Kaisen ura futomaki
Tuna, salmon and avocado with tobiko giant inside-out roll
(2 rolls / 16–20 pieces)

Oyako temari sushi
Smoked salmon and salmon roe hand-ball sushi
(multiply recipe by 4 to make 16 pieces)

Ebi temari sushi
Prawn with lumpfish roe hand-ball sushi
(multiply recipe by 4 to make 16 pieces)

A feast for 8

Ebi tem cha-soba sushi with ume-su sauce
Prawn tempura and green-tea soba-noodle sushi with Japanese plum sauce
(2 rolls / 16–20 pieces)

Shime saba and shiso ura hosomaki
Marinated mackerel and shiso leaves with white sesame seeds small inside-out roll
(4–6 rolls / 24–36 pieces)

Kakiage futomaki
Mixed vegetable and prawn tempura giant roll
(2 rolls / 16–20 pieces)

Yaki saba bo sushi
Grilled mackerel bo sushi
(2 bo sushi / 10–12 pieces)

An indulgent seafood dinner for 4

Clam miso soup
(serves 4)

Tuna tataki and yakumi
Seared tuna with Japanese herb sauce
(serves 4)

Classic kaisen chirashi sushi
Seafood chirashi sushi
(serves 4)

A vegetarian meal for 4

Kuro goma-ae
Green beans with black sesame sauce
(serves 4)

Umeboshi and cucumber with shiso temaki
Japanese pickled plum and cucumber with shiso leaves hand roll
(4 hand rolls)

Classic vegetable futomaki
Dashi-maki tamago, braised shiitake mushrooms, carrots and cucumber giant roll
(2 rolls / 16–20 pieces)

A hand-roll dinner for 4

Creamy scallops tobiko temaki
Scallops and frying-fish roe with avocado sauce hand roll
(4 rolls)

Ebi furai chilli-mayo temaki
Deep-fried prawn, Japanese panko breadcrumb and sweet chilli-mayo hand roll
(4 rolls)

Cucumber, wakame and prawn salad with Japanese mustard and sesame sauce
(serves 4)

An elegant dinner for 2

Sea bream and shiso temari
Sea bream and shiso hand-ball sushi
(4 temari sushi)

Hotate temari sushi
Scallop and chives hand-ball sushi
(4 temari sushi)

Ebi temari sushi
Prawn with lumpfish roe hand-ball sushi
(4 temari sushi)

Tai sashimi with mikan chilli sauce and mizuna
Sea-bream sashimi with satsuma chilli sauce and mizuna leaves
(serves 2 as a main)

A vegetarian meal for 2

Goma-ae inari sushi
Spinach with white sesame inari sushi
(6 inari)

Hijiki chirashi sushi
Braised sea vegetable and shiitake mushrooms chirashi sushi
(serves 4 – save some for lunch the following day!)

Acknowledgements

There are many people who have helped with ingredients and equipment in the course of this book who I would like to thank, most notably *Clearspring* and Kai Shun Knives.

This book has been spurred on by the support of my family both here and in Japan. Thank you to:

My best teacher, my mother, Yoshimi, in Yamanashi. We have always talked about food, and you have nurtured my passion since I was young. Thank you for risking the international post to send me beautiful ceramics from home, including some handmade Yoshimi originals! I am so glad they appear in this book. お母さん、感謝の気持ちで一杯です。

My father, Tatsuro, who sadly is no longer with us, for encouraging my curiosity by bringing me culinary treats from Tokyo, and for taking me to amazing restaurants that helped me to develop my palate in beautiful surroundings.

My mother-in-law, Gillian: you have become a dear friend as well as being wonderfully patient in advising me on and editing my recipes.

Alex, my husband and chief recipe tester, for all your honest and trusting support.

My brother, Tatsuya, and his wife, Aimi. My father-in-law, Karl, and brother-in-law, Douglas.

Chef Curtis: you made me a chef in the USA when I was still at culinary school and trusted me with your knives and Chicago team. I am still so grateful for how much you taught me; and inspired by your commitment to the discovery of new dishes.

Master sushi chef Mr Tokunaga, and master soba-noodle chef Mr Sekizawa: I feel privileged to have learnt dedication to the Japanese culinary arts from you.

Linda Carter: for making a hard-working chef's hands look presentable.

Everyone at Fig Tree and Penguin: Juliet Annan and Sophie Missing for all your support, trust and enthusiasm, and Ellie Smith and Alice Burkle.

Everyone else who worked so hard on this book: my copy-editor, Caroline Pretty; Jan Stevens, who tested all the recipes; and Giulia Garbin for the lovely design and illustrations.

Keiko Oikawa: your photos are inspiring and I am so pleased that you could work on this book. It has been great talking about all things food and I am glad to have met someone with your sensitivity for Japanese dishes.

My agent, Adrian Sington, and also Charlotte Ridge at DCD Media, for your hard work.

Finally, thank you to all my students and friends, past and present. I have enjoyed teaching you and I have learnt much from you all too. My first students and dearest friends, Amanda Mann and Stephanie Scull: thank you for your support and belief in me over the years.

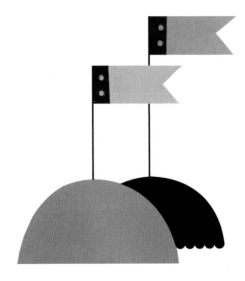

Index

A
abura-age 17
    inari sushi 121, 122
aonori 17
    una-q aonori ura hosomaki 45–6
avocados:
    avocado with black sesame seeds small
        inside-out roll 38–9
    Japanese grilled eel and avocado pressed
        sushi 96
    salmon, crabmeat, avocado and chives
        giant roll 54–5
    scallops and flying-fish roe with avocado
        sauce hand roll 81, 83
    tuna, salmon and avocado with tobiko
        giant inside-out roll 60–1
awase dashi 154–5

B
beans: green beans with black sesame
    sauce 137
bo sushi 69
    shime saba bo sushi 71–2
    yaki saba bo sushi 70
bonito:
    bonito-flake stock 156
    dried kelp and bonito-flake stock 154
breadcrumbs: deep-fried prawn, Japanese
    panko breadcrumb and sweet chilli-mayo
    hand roll 78, 80
buckwheat noodle sushi *see* soba sushi

C
carrots: dashi-maki tamago, braised shiitake
    mushrooms, carrots and cucumber giant
    roll 50–2
ceviche: Japanese-style sea-bream ceviche
    hand roll 80–1
chilli:
    deep-fried prawn, Japanese panko
        breadcrumb and sweet chilli-mayo
        hand roll 78, 80
    satsuma chilli sauce 132
chirashi sushi 103
    classic kaisen chirashi sushi 104
    hana chirashi sushi 105
    hijiki chirashi sushi 108–9
    una-q chirashi sushi 108
chives:
    natto with chives small roll 33–4
    salmon, crabmeat, avocado and chives
        giant roll 54–5
    scallop and chives hand-ball sushi 90
clam miso soup 142
coriander: sea bream and coriander with
    white sesame seeds small inside-out roll 39, 42
crab 150–51
    crabmeat and king prawn mini pressed
        sushi 97, 99
    mixed seafood and vegetable chirashi
        sushi 105
    salmon, crabmeat, avocado and chives
        giant roll 54–5

cucumbers:

cucumber small roll 30–1

cucumber and squid salad with sanbai-su
dressing 140

cucumber, wakame and prawn salad
with Japanese mustard and sesame
sauce 139

dashi-maki tamago, braised shiitake
mushrooms, carrots and cucumber
giant roll 50–2

eel, dashi-maki tamago and cucumber
with white sesame seeds giant inside-
out roll 64

grilled eel and cucumber with powdered
seaweed small inside-out roll 45–6

grilled eel, Japanese omelette and
cucumber soba-noodle sushi 112–13

Japanese grilled eel and cucumber
chirashi sushi 108

Japanese pickled plums and cucumber
with shiso leaves hand roll 76, 78

poached tuna wasabi mayo, cucumber
and mizuna with black sesame seeds
giant inside-out roll 65–6

D

daikon 17

daikon oshinko maki 32–3

dashi 153

awase dashi 154

katsuo dashi 156

kombu dashi 156

niboshi dashi 155

shiitake-mushroom dashi 157

dashi-maki tamago:

dashi-maki tamago, braised shiitake
mushrooms, carrots and cucumber
giant roll 50–2

eel, dashi-maki tamago and cucumber
with white sesame seeds giant inside-
out roll 64

mixed seafood and vegetable chirashi
sushi 105

dressings: sanbai-su dressing 140

E

ebi furai chilli-mayo temaki 78, 80

ebi temari sushi 86

ebi tem cha-soba sushi with ume-su sauce
113–14, 116

edamame 17

eels:

eel, dashi-maki tamago and cucumber
with white sesame seeds giant inside-
out roll 64

grilled eel and cucumber with powdered
seaweed small inside-out roll 45–6

grilled eel, Japanese omelette and
cucumber soba-noodle sushi 112–13

Japanese grilled eel and avocado pressed
sushi 96

Japanese grilled eel and cucumber
chirashi sushi 108

eggs see omelettes

F

flying-fish roe:

scallops and flying-fish roe with avocado
sauce hand roll 81, 83

tuna, salmon and avocado with tobiko giant
inside-out roll 60–1

furikake 17

futomaki 49

classic seafood futomaki 54–5

classic vegetable futomaki 50–2

kakiage futomaki 55–6

G

gari 17

genmai miso 17

giant inside-out roll *see* ura futomaki

giant roll *see* futomaki

ginger:

   pickled ginger 13

   yakumi 130, 132

goma-ae:

   goma-ae inari sushi 124

   kuro goma-ae 137

green beans with black sesame sauce 137

green tea: prawn tempura and green-tea

   soba-noodle sushi with Japanese plum

   sauce 113–14, 116

H

hand roll *see* temaki

hand-ball sushi *see* temari sushi

hatcho miso 17

herring 148

hijiki 17

hijiki chirashi sushi 108–9

hijiki inari sushi 123

hosomaki 29

   daikon oshinko maki 32–3

   kappa maki 30–1

   natto negi maki 33–4

   tekka maki 31–2

hotate temari sushi 90

I

ichiban dashi 154

ikura 17

inari sushi 121–2

   goma-ae inari sushi 124

   hijiki inari sushi 123

inside-out roll *see* ura futomaki; ura hosomaki

K

kaisen ura futomaki 60–1

kakiage futomaki 55–6

kani and ebi oshi sushi 97, 99

kappa maki 30–31

katsuo dashi 156

katsuobushi 17

kelp:

   dried kelp and bonito-flake stock 154–5

   dried kelp stock 156

kinshi tamago 17

kombu 17

kombu dashi 17, 156

kome miso 17

koryori 135

   cucumber, wakame and prawn salad with

     Japanese mustard and sesame sauce 139

   kuro goma-ae 137

   sunomono 140

kuro goma-ae 137

L

lumpfish roe: prawn with lumpfish roe

   hand-ball sushi 86

M

mackerel 148

   grilled mackerel bo sushi 70

   marinated mackerel bo sushi 71–2

   marinated mackerel and shiso leaves with

     white sesame seeds small inside-out

     roll 42–4

masago 17

masu sushi 100

mayonnaise:

   deep-fried prawn, Japanese panko

     breadcrumb and sweet chilli-mayo

     hand roll 78, 80

mayonnaise (*cont.*)

poached tuna wasabi mayo, cucumber and mizuna with black sesame seeds giant inside-out roll 65–6

mirin 18

miso 17

clam miso soup 142

mizuna 17

poached tuna wasabi mayo, cucumber and mizuna with black sesame seeds giant inside-out roll 65–6

sea-bream sashimi with satsuma chilli sauce and mizuna leaves 132

mugi miso 17

mushrooms:

braised sea vegetable and shiitake mushrooms chirashi sushi 108–9

dashi-maki tamago, braised shiitake mushrooms, carrots and cucumber giant roll 50–2

dried shiitake-mushroom stock 157

mustard: Japanese mustard and sesame sauce 139

N

natto 17

natto negi maki 33–4

niban dashi 155

niboshi dashi 155

noodle sushi *see* soba sushi

nori 18

O

okra: marinated tuna with okra and shiso leaves soba sushi 116–17

omelettes:

dashi-maki tamago, braised shiitake mushrooms, carrots and cucumber giant roll 50–2

eel, dashi-maki tamago and cucumber with white-sesame giant inside-out roll 64

grilled eel, Japanese omelette and cucumber soba-noodle sushi 112–13

mixed seafood and vegetable chirashi sushi 105

oshi sushi 95

kani and ebi oshi sushi 97, 99

masu sushi 100

unagi and avocado oshi sushi 96

oyako temari sushi 88

P

panko 18

deep-fried prawn, Japanese panko breadcrumb and sweet chilli-mayo hand roll 78, 80

pickled ginger 13

pickled Japanese radish small roll 32–3

plums:

Japanese pickled plums and cucumber with shiso leaves hand roll 76, 78

prawn tempura and green-tea soba-noodle sushi with Japanese plum sauce 113–14, 116

ponzu sauce 129–30

prawns 149–50

crabmeat and king prawn mini pressed sushi 97, 99

cucumber, wakame and prawn salad with Japanese mustard and sesame sauce 139

deep-fried prawn, Japanese panko breadcrumb and sweet chilli-mayo hand roll 78, 80

mixed seafood and vegetable chirashi sushi 105

mixed vegetable and prawn tempura
    giant roll 55–6
prawn with lumpfish roe hand-ball sushi 86
prawn tempura and green-tea soba-noodle
    sushi with Japanese plum sauce 113–14, 116
seafood chirashi sushi 104
pressed sushi *see* oshi sushi

R
radish: pickled Japanese radish small roll 32–3
red snapper 148
rice 18, 25
    inari sushi 122
    measurements 15
    sushi brown rice 27
    sushi rice 26

S
saikyo miso 18
sake 18
salmon 145–7
    mixed seafood and vegetable chirashi
        sushi 105
    salmon, crabmeat, avocado and chives
        giant roll 54–5
    seafood chirashi sushi 104
    smoked salmon and salmon roe hand-ball
        sushi 88
    tuna, salmon and avocado with tobiko
        giant inside-out roll 60–1
sanbai-su dressing 140
sardines 148
    dried baby-sardine stock 155
sashimi 127
    salmon sashimi with ponzu sauce 129–30
    tai sashimi with mikan chilli sauce and
        mizuna 132
    tuna tataki and yakumi 130, 132

satsuma chilli sauce 132
sauces:
    black sesame sauce 137
    Japanese herb sauce 130, 132
    ponzu sauce 129
    satsuma chilli sauce 132
scallops 151
    creamy scallops tobiko temaki 81, 83
    scallop and chives hand-ball sushi 90
    scallops and flying-fish roe with avocado
        sauce hand roll 81, 83
    seafood chirashi sushi 104
sea bass 148
sea bream 149
    Japanese-style sea-bream ceviche hand
        roll 80–81
    sea bream and coriander with white
        sesame seeds small inside-out roll 39, 42
    sea-bream sashimi with satsuma chilli
        sauce and mizuna leaves 132
    sea bream and shiso hand-ball sushi 89
    seafood chirashi sushi 104
sea vegetable:
    braised sea vegetable and shiitake
        mushrooms chirashi sushi 108–9
    sea-vegetable inari sushi 123
    see also aonori; kelp; wakame
sesame seeds 18
    avocado with black sesame seeds small
        inside-out roll 38–9
    eel, dashi-maki tamago and cucumber
        with white sesame seeds giant inside-
        out roll 64
    green beans with black sesame sauce 137
    Japanese mustard and sesame sauce 139
    marinated mackerel and shiso leaves with
        white sesame seeds small inside-out
        roll 42–4

sesame seeds (*cont.*)

poached tuna wasabi mayo, cucumber
and mizuna with black sesame seeds
giant inside-out roll 65–6

sea bream and coriander with white
sesame seeds small inside-out roll 39, 42

spinach with white sesame inari sushi 124

shari 26

shime saba bo sushi 71–2

shime saba and shiso ura hosomaki 42–4

shiso 18, 42

Japanese pickled plums and cucumber
with shiso leaves hand roll 76, 78

marinated mackerel and shiso leaves with
white sesame seeds small inside-out
roll 42–4

marinated tuna with okra and shiso
leaves soba sushi 116–17

sea bream and shiso hand-ball sushi 89

trout with shiso leaves 100

yakumi 130, 132

shiitake mushrooms:

braised sea vegetable and shiitake
mushrooms chirashi sushi 108–9

dashi-maki tamago, braised shiitake
mushrooms, carrots and cucumber
giant roll 50–52

dried shiitake-mushroom stock 157

small inside-out roll *see* ura hosomaki

small roll *see* hosomaki

soba noodles 18

soba sushi 111

ebi tem cha-soba sushi with ume-su sauce
113–14, 116

tsuke-maguro, okura and shiso soba sushi
116–17

unagi, tamago and cucumber soba sushi
112–13

soup: clam miso soup 142

soy sauce 13

spinach with white sesame inari sushi 124

spring onions:

yakumi 130, 132

squid: cucumber and squid salad with
sanbai-su dressing 140

stock 153

bonito-flake stock 156

dried baby-sardine stock 155

dried kelp and bonito-flake stock 154

dried kelp stock 156

dried shiitake-mushroom stock 157

su meshi 26

sunomono 140

sushi rice 18, 25, 26

inari sushi 122

measurements 15

sushi brown rice 27

sushi-su 18, 26–7

T

tai sashimi with mikan chilli sauce and
mizuna 132

tamago:

dashi-maki tamago, braised shiitake
mushrooms, carrots and cucumber
giant roll 50–2

eel, dashi-maki tamago and cucumber
with white sesame seeds giant inside-
out roll 64

mixed seafood and vegetable chirashi
sushi 105

unagi, tamago and cucumber soba sushi
112–13

tamari soy sauce 18

tea: prawn tempura and green-tea soba-noodle
sushi with Japanese plum sauce 113–14, 116

tekka maki 31–2
temaki 75
    creamy scallops tobiko temaki 81, 83
    ebi furai chilli-mayo temaki 78, 80
    sea-bream ceviche temaki 80–1
    umeboshi and cucumber with shiso
      temaki 76, 78
temari sushi 85
    ebi temari sushi 86
    hotate temari sushi 90
    oyako temari sushi 88
    sea bream and shiso temari 89
tempura:
    mixed vegetable and prawn tempura
      giant roll 55–6
    prawn tempura and green-tea soba-noodle
      sushi with Japanese plum sauce
      113–14, 116
tobiko 18
    scallops and flying-fish roe with avocado
      sauce hand roll 81, 83
    tuna, salmon and avocado with tobiko
      giant inside-out roll 60–1
trout with shiso leaves pressed sushi 100
tsuke-maguro, okura and shiso soba
    sushi 116–17
tsuma 18
tuna 147–8
    marinated tuna with okra and shiso
      leaves soba sushi 116–17
    mixed seafood and vegetable chirashi
      sushi 105
    poached tuna wasabi mayo, cucumber
      and mizuna with black sesame
      seeds giant inside-out roll 65–6
    seafood chirashi sushi 104
    seared tuna with Japanese herb sauce
      130, 132

tuna, salmon and avocado with tobiko
    giant inside-out roll 60–1
tuna and wasabi small roll 31–2

U
umeboshi 18
    umeboshi and cucumber with shiso
      temaki 76, 78
unagi 18
    unagi and avocado oshi sushi 96
    unagi, tamago and cucumber soba sushi
      112–13
    unagi tamago cucumber ura futomaki 64
    una-q aonori ura hosomaki 45–6
    una-q chirashi sushi 108
ura futomaki 59
    kaisen ura futomaki 60–61
    tuna salad ura futomaki 65–6
unagi tamago cucumber ura futomaki 64
ura hosomaki 37
    sea bream and coriander ura hosomaki
      39, 42
    shime saba and shiso ura hosomaki 42–4
    simple avocado ura hosomaki 38–9
    una-q aonori ura hosomaki 45–6

V
vinegar: sushi-su 26–7

W
wakame 18
wakame
    cucumber, wakame and prawn salad with
      Japanese mustard and sesame sauce 139
wasabi 13, 18
    poached tuna wasabi mayo, cucumber
      and mizuna with black sesame seeds
      giant inside-out roll 65–6

wasabi (*cont.*)
    tuna and wasabi small roll 31–2

Y
yaki saba bo sushi 70
yakumi 130, 132